RUDOLF STEINER

The Roots of Education

Anthroposophic Press

*The publisher wishes to acknowledge the inspiration
and support of Connie and Robert Dulaney*

❖ ❖ ❖

These lectures are contained in the German *Anthroposophische Pädagogik und ihre Voraussetzungen* (vol. no. 309 in the Bibliographical Survey) published by Rudolf Steiner Verlag, Dornach, Switzerland. Translated from shorthand reports unrevised by the lecturer; first published in English in 1968 (translator unknown). Revised by Helen Fox in 1982. The lectures have been checked against the German text and revised by Anthroposophic Press for this edition.

Published by Anthroposophic Press
3390 Route 9, Hudson, NY 12534

Library of Congress Cataloging-in-Publication Data to come

Steiner, Rudolf, 1861–1925.
    [Anthroposophische Pädagogik und ihre Voraussetzungen. English]
    The roots of education / Rudolf Steiner.
        p. cm.— (Foundations of Waldorf education ; 19)
    Five lectures given in Apr. 1924.
    Includes bibliographical references.
    ISBN 0-88010-415-5 (paper)
    1. Education. 2. Anthroposophy. I. Title. II. Series.
LB775.S7A413 1997
370'.1--dc21   97-35327
                                                                     CIP

10 9 8 7 6 5 4 3 2 1

Printed in the United States of America

895

THE ROOTS OF EDUCATION

WITHDRAWN

[XIX]

FOUNDATIONS OF WALDORF EDUCATION

Contents

A new education requires a new knowledge of the whole human being in body, soul, and spirit. The change of teeth signals the end of the first stage of childhood. Soul and spirit descend into a body provided by inheritance, which is used as the model for the "second" human being. During the first stage the child is a sense organ that perceives moral influences. The influence of the teacher's temperament.

The goal of Waldorf education is to reveal new methods of teaching. The power of spiritual perception for understanding children and adults. Sleeping and waking. The seasons reflected in the human being. Thinking as an etheric "grasping." Materialistic ideas and insomnia. Psychic influences and physical effects.

Memory before and after the change of teeth. The physical and etheric bodies. The etheric body and sculpting. The astral body and music. The I-being and speech. The musical scale and the human body. The teacher as therapist. Doctors and the school. Teaching letters.

LECTURE 4

The sense organization and moral development at the change of teeth. Mathematics begins with the whole. The child's natural religious impulse. The need for images after seven. The need to feel a connection with destiny after fourteen. The child's relationship with the world.

LECTURE 5

The three divisions of the middle stage of childhood. Nature and history. Children after puberty go into life. The experience of immortality. Punishment. Reading the child. The need for a living experience of one another today. Moon and Sun forces in the plant world. Spiritual science reveals the unity of the human being with the world.

Introduction

In this series of five lectures, given just eleven months before his death, Rudolf Steiner finds a variety of ways to call for a change in the practice of teaching. This will depend on how the teacher is able to view the developing human being and the curriculum that responds to the child's changing needs.

Steiner ended his lectures in Stuttgart by saying:

> What is our most intense suffering? By trying to characterize our education I repeatedly had to point out that we stand with reverent awe before the human I-being placed in the world by divine powers helping to develop that I. The human I is not truly understood unless it is understood in spirit; it is denied when understood only in matter. It is primarily the I that has suffered because of our contemporary materialistic life, because of ignorance, because of the wrong concept of the human I. This is primarily due to the fact that—while we have hammered away at perception of matter and at activity in matter—spirit has been shattered, and with it the I.[1]

---

1. *The Essentials of Education*, pp. 78–79. Many of the themes presented in *The Essentials of Education* were reformulated by Steiner in these lectures in Bern. The reader may refer to the introduction in the new translation of *The Essentials of Education* for a more complete overview of the content.

In Bern, he begins *The Roots of Education* with a similar plea to counter materialism in our time, and this aspect needs our further efforts today. Many who come to Waldorf education have a sense of the more overt aspects of materialism—self-worth defined by one's possessions and social position, for example. Yet there are more subtle aspects of materialism that should be discussed.

Whenever considerations are frozen in time, we can succumb to materialism. This might assume the form of how one's child or student is doing *now.* When something is divorced from context, it also tends to accentuate one-sidedness and opens doors to materialism. For example, one may view every issue purely from a financial, a pedagogical, or a legal perspective. When issues are constrained by rigid frames—for example, when people are seen as objects in space without consideration of time—we have increased materialism.

By contrast, in these lectures Rudolf Steiner asks us to look at the whole lifespan, to place what happens in childhood in the context of a series of phases that stretches into adult life. His treatment of almost every issue in education is expansive; again and again, he looks at questions from a longitudinal perspective. Also, the process of characterization, rather than defining, calls on the reader to exercise new flexibility in thinking, and to develop the ability to view things from various sides. Steiner seems to ask continually: Now that you have understood it from this point of view, let us consider the question from another side.

"Anthroposophy is often criticized for wanting to speak of spirit as well as soul" (page 13). Our culture seems to have embraced one or the other—soul or spirit, but not both. Why is it that so many people deny either spirit or soul? It is as if the grip of polarity is too strong. In working with modern materialism, it will be increasingly important to really discover what is meant by a *threefold human constitution*, one that includes body, soul, and spirit. These lectures give us an opportunity to engage in that expansion.

TORIN M. FINSER, Ph.D.
Director, Waldorf Program
Antioch Graduate School, Keene, New Hampshire

Lecture One

BERN, APRIL 13, 1924

New Education and the Whole Human Being

Here in Bern, I have spoken to you often about anthroposophy in general. And it is a special pleasure to be able now to speak to you in the spirit of anthroposophy about education—the sphere of life that must lie closest to the human heart. We must develop an art of education that can lead us out of the social chaos into which we have fallen during the last few years and decades. Our chances of overcoming this chaos are very slight. In fact, one is tempted to say that there is no escaping this chaos unless we find a way to bring spirituality into human souls through education, so that human beings may find a way to progress and to further the evolution of civilization out of the spirit itself.

We feel confident that this is the right way to proceed, because in our hearts we know that the world is created in spirit and arises from spirit. Therefore, human creation will be fruitful only when it springs from the fountainhead of spirit itself. To achieve such fruitful creation from spirit, however, people must also be educated and taught in the spirit. I believe that anthroposophy in fact has much to say about the nature of education and teaching, therefore, it gives me great satisfaction that I can present these lectures here.

There are many all over the world who feel that a new impetus of some kind is needed in education and teaching. It is true that the nineteenth century was full of progressive ideas and much was done to further schooling and education. However, a recent tendency of our civilization has been that individuals are seldom brought into touch with their own humanity. For many centuries we have been able to record the most wonderful progress in the realm of natural science and in its resulting technology.

We have also seen that a certain worldview has gradually crystallized out of that scientific progress. The world as a whole—which includes the human being—seems to be viewed exclusively in terms of what the senses tell us about natural phenomena, and what the intellect, which is related to the brain, tells us about the realm of the senses. Nevertheless, all of our recently acquired knowledge about the natural world does not, in fact, lead us to the human being; this is not clearly recognized today. Although many people feel this to be the situation, they are unprepared to acknowledge that—regardless of all that the modern age has provided us in terms of information about the natural world—we are still no closer to understanding the human being.

This impossibility is most likely to be felt when we attempt to understand the growing human being, the child. We sense a barrier between the teacher and the child. Anthroposophy, which is based on a real and comprehensive understanding of the human being, would hear this heartfelt appeal coming from all sides—not by establishing theories on education, but by showing men and women as teachers how to enter the school's practical life. Anthroposophic education is really the practical life of the school, and our lectures should provide practical details about how to deal with the various details of teaching.

Something else must come first, however; for if we were to begin by speaking of practical details in this way, then the spirit that gives birth to all this could not reveal itself. Therefore, you must kindly permit me to speak today of this spirit of anthroposophic education as a kind of introduction. What we have to say about it will be based on a comprehensive, truly penetrating knowledge of the human being—the active force of anthroposophy in education.

A penetrating knowledge of the human being—what does this mean to us? If a growing human being, a child, stands before us, it is not enough, as I have said, to make certain rules for teaching and educating this child, merely conforming to rules as one would when dealing with a technical problem. This will not lead to good teaching. We must bring an inner fire and enthusiasm to our work; we must have impulses that are not transmitted intellectually from teacher to child according to certain rules, but ones that pass intimately from teacher to child. An educator's whole being must be at work, not just the thinking person; the person who feels and the person who wills must also play their roles.

Recently, the thinking and worldview of natural science have taken hold of people more deeply and closer to the marrow than they like to think. Even those not specifically trained as scientists think, feel, and act scientifically. This is not acceptable for teachers, since scientific thinking provides an understanding of only one member of the whole human being—the physical body, or body of the senses. But this is only one member of the entire human being, and anthroposophy shows us that when we have genuine knowledge of the human being, we see that the human being possesses three clearly distinguished members—physical body, soul, and spirit.

We see the whole human being only when we have enough wisdom and knowledge to recognize the soul's true nature as clearly as we recognize the physical body. We must also be able to recognize the human spirit as an individual being. Nevertheless, the connections among the body, soul, and spirit in the child are not the same as in the adult; and it is precisely a loosening of the connection with the physical body that allows us to observe the soul and spirit of the child as the greatest wonder of knowledge and practical life in human existence.

The First Stage of Childhood

Let's look for a moment at the tiny child and see how that child is born into the world. Here we see a genuinely magical process at work. We see how spirit, springing from the innermost being of the little child, flows into undefined features, chaotic movements, and every action, which seem still disjointed and disconnected. Order and form come into the child's eyes, facial expressions and physical movements, and the child's features become increasingly expressive. In the eyes and other features, the spirit manifests, working from within to the surface, and the soul—which permeates the entire body—manifests.

When we look at these things with a serious, unbiased attitude, we see how they come about by observing the growing child; in this way we may gaze reverently into the wonders and enigmas of cosmic and human existence. As we watch in this way while the child develops, we learn to distinguish three clearly differentiated stages. The only reason such stages are not generally distinguished is because such discernment depends on deep, intimate knowledge; and people today, with their crude scientific concepts, are not going to trouble themselves by acquiring this kind of intimate knowledge.

Soul and Spirit Build the "Second" Human Being

The first significant change in a child's life occurs around the seventh year when the second teeth appear. The outer physical process of the change of teeth is itself very interesting. First we have the baby teeth, then the others force their way through as the first are pushed out. A superficial look at this process will see no farther than the actual change of teeth. But when we look into it more deeply (through means I will describe later in these lectures) we discover that this transformation can be observed throughout the child's body, though more delicately than the actual change of teeth. The change of teeth is the most physical and basic expression of a subtle process that in fact occurs throughout the body.

What really happens? Anyone can see how the human organism develops. We cut our nails, our hair, and we find that our skin flakes off. This demonstrates how physical substance is cast off from the surface as it is constantly pushed out from within. This pushing from within—which we observe in the change of teeth—is present throughout the whole human body. More exacting knowledge shows us that indeed the child gradually forced out the body received through inheritance; it was cast out. The first teeth are forced out, and likewise the child's whole initial body is forced out.

At the change of teeth, a child stands before us with a body that—in contrast to the body at birth—is entirely formed anew. The body from birth has been cast out as are the first teeth, and a new body is formed. What is the nature of this more intimate process? The child's first body was inherited. It is the result of a collaboration between the father and mother, so to speak, and it is formed from the earthly physical conditions. But, just what is this physical body? It is the model that the Earth provides to the person as a model for true development as a human being. The soul and spirit aspect of a human being descends from a realm of soul and spirit where it lived prior to conception and birth. Before we became earthly beings in a physical body, we were all beings of soul and spirit in a soul and spirit realm. What we are given by our parents through inherited physical substance unites in embryonic life with what descends from a higher realm as pure spirit and soul. Spirit and soul take hold of the physical body, whose origin is in the stream of inheritance. This physical body becomes its model, and on this model an entirely new human organism is formed, while the inherited organism is forced out.

Thus, when we consider a child between birth and the change of teeth we can say that the physical body's existence is due to physical inheritance alone. But, two other forces then combine to work on this physical body. First is the force of those elements the human being brought with it to Earth; the second is assimilated from the matter and substance of the Earth itself. By the time the teeth change, the human being has fashioned a second body modeled after the inherited body, and that second body is the product of the human soul and spirit.

Having arrived at such conclusions by observing the human being more intimately, one will naturally be aware of objections that may be raised; such objections are obvious. One is bound to ask: Can't you see that a likeness to the parents often appears after the change of teeth—that, therefore, a person is still subject to the laws of inheritance, even after the change of teeth? One could raise a number of similar objections.

Let's consider just this one: We have a model that comes from the stream of inheritance. On this model the spirit and soul develop the second human being. But when something is built from a model we don't expect to find a complete dissimilarity to the model; thus, it should be clear that the human spirit and soul use the model's existence to build up the second human organism in its likeness.

Nevertheless, when you can perceive and recognize what really occurs, you discover something. Certain children come into their second organism between nine and eleven, and this second body is almost identical to the initial, inherited organism. With other children, one may notice a dissimilarity between the second organism and the first, and it is clear that something very different is working its way from the center of their being. In truth, we see every variation between these two extremes. While the human spirit and soul aspect is developing the second organism, it tries most of all to conform to the being it brings with it from the realm of spirit and soul.

A conflict thus arises between what is intended to built as the second organism and what the first organism received through inheritance. Depending on whether thy have had a stronger or weaker spiritual and soul existence (in the following lectures we shall see why this is), human beings can either give their second organism an individual form that is strongly impregnated with soul forces, or, if they descend from the spiritual world with weaker forces, stay as closely as possible to the model.

Consider what we must deal with to educate children during the first period of life between birth and the change of teeth. We are inspired with great reverence when we see how divine spiritual forces work down from supersensible realms! We witness them working daily and weekly, from month to month and year to year, during the first phases of children's lives, and we see how such work carries them through to forming a second individual body. In education we participate in this work of spirit and soul; for human physical existence, we continue what divine spiritual forces began. We participate in divine labor.

The Child as a Sense Organ

These matters require more than strictly intellectual understanding; one's whole being must comprehend them. Indeed, when we are brought face to face with the creative forces of the world, we may sense the magnitude of our task in education, especially during the early years. But I would like to point out to you that the way spirit and soul enter the work of creating a second human organism shows us that, in the child, the formation of the body, the activity of the soul, and the creation of the spirit are a unity. Whatever happens while forming a new organism and pushing out the old involves a unity of spirit, soul, and body.

Consequently, children reveal themselves very differently than do adults. We may observe this clearly in individual instances. As adults, when we eat something sweet, it is the tongue and palate that perceive its sweetness; a little later, the experience of sweetness ceases when the sweet substance has gone into another part of the body. As adults, we do not follow it farther with our taste. This is very different for a child, in whom taste permeates the whole organism; children do not taste only with the tongue and palate but with the whole organism. The sweetness is drawn throughout the organism. In fact, the whole child is a sensory organ.

In essence, what is a sensory organ? Let's consider the human eye. Colors make an impression on the eye. If we properly consider what is involved in human seeing, one has to say that will and perception are one in the human eye. The surface is involved—the periphery of the human being. During the first years of life, however, between birth and the change of teeth, such activity permeates the whole organism, though in a delicate way. The child's whole organism views itself as one all-inclusive sense organ. This is why all impressions from the environment affect children very differently than they would an adult. An expression of the soul element in the human being—the element of human morality—is occurring in the environment, and this can be seen with the eye.

The Effects of the Teacher's Temperament on Children

Subconsciously—even unconsciously—children have a delicate and intimate capacity for perceiving what is expressed in every movement and act of those around them. If a choleric person expresses fury in the presence of a child and allows the child to see this in the unconscious way I described, then, believe me, we are very mistaken to believe that the child sees only the outer activity. Children have a clear impression of what is contained within these moral acts, even when it is an unconscious impression. Sense impressions of the eye are also unconscious. Impressions that are not strictly sensory impressions, but expressions of the moral and soul life, flow into a child exactly the way colors flow into the eye, because the child's organism is a sense organ.

This organism, however, has such a delicate structure that every impression permeates all of it. The first impression a child receives from any moral manifestation is a soul impression. For a child, however, the soul always works down into the bodily nature. Whether it be fear or joy and delight that a child experiences in the environment, all this passes—not crudely but in a subtle and delicate way—into the processes of growth, circulation, and digestion. Children who live in constant terror of what may come their way as expressions of fury and anger from a choleric person, experience something in the soul that immediately penetrates the breathing, the circulation of the blood, and even the digestive activities. This is tremendously significant. In childhood we cannot speak only of physical education, because soul education also means educating the body; everything in the soul element is metamorphosed into the body—it becomes body.

We will realize the significance of this only when, through genuine knowledge of the human being, we do more than merely look at children and imprint certain educational maxims on them, and instead consider all of human earthly life. This is more difficult than merely observing children. We may record observations regarding memory, thinking powers, sensory functions of the eye, ear, and so on, but such records are made for the moment or, at most, for a short while. But this has not helped us in any way toward true knowledge of the human being as such.

When we look at a plant, something is already contained there in the seed that takes root and, after a long time, will appear as blossom and fruit. Similarly, in children before the change of teeth, when the bodily nature is susceptible to the soul's influences, there are seeds of happiness and unhappiness, health and sickness, which will affect all of life until death. As teachers and educators, whatever we allow to flow into children during their first phase of life will work down into the blood, breathing, and digestion; it is like a seed that may come to fruition only in the form of health or sickness when they are forty or fifty years old. It is in fact true that the way educators act toward the little child creates the predispositions for happiness or unhappiness, sickness or health.

This is particularly noticeable when we observe in detail the effects of teachers on the children, based on actual life events. These phenomena may be observed just as well as the phenomena of botany or physics in laboratories, but we seldom see this. Let us consider individual examples. Let us consider, for instance, the teacher's relationship to a child in school. Consider the teacher's temperament. We may know that, due to temperament, a choleric teacher may be energetic, but also quick-tempered and easily angered. A melancholic teacher may be the kind of person who withdraws into the self—an introvert who is self-occupied and avoids the world. A sanguine teacher may be quick to receive outer impressions, flitting from one impression to the next. Or, we may find a phlegmatic person who allows things to slide, someone indifferent to everything, who remains unaffected by outer impressions, generally gliding over things.

Let's imagine for the moment that a teachers' training college did nothing to moderate these temperaments and prepare teachers to function well in the school life—that these temperaments were allowed full and total expression with no restraint. The choleric temperament—let us imagine that, before the change of teeth, a child is exposed to a choleric temperament. If a teacher or educator lets loose with a temperament of this kind, it permanently affects the child's soul, leaving its mark on the circulatory system and all that constitutes the inner rhythmic life. Such effects do not initially penetrate very deeply; really, they are only there in seed, but this seed grows and grows, as all seeds do. It sometimes happens that, at forty or fifty years of age, circulatory disorders of the rhythmic system appear as a direct result of a teacher's unrestrained choleric temperament. Indeed, we do not educate children only for childhood, but for their whole earthly existence and even, as we shall see later, for the time beyond.

Or, let's imagine a melancholic giving rein to that particular temperament—someone who was not motivated during teacher training to harmonize it and find an appropriate way to channel it into working with children. Such teachers succumb to their own melancholy in their interactions with children. But by living, feeling, and thinking such inner melancholy, such a person continually withholds from children exactly what should flow from teacher to child—that is, *warmth*. This warmth, which is so often missing in education, acts first as a warmth of soul, and then passes into the body, primarily into the digestive system. This quickens the seed of certain tendencies that appear later in life as all kinds of disorders and blood diseases.

Or consider the phlegmatic, a person who is indifferent to interactions with the child. A very peculiar relationship arises between them—not exactly a coldness, but an extremely watery element is active in the soul realm between the child and such a teacher. The foundation is not strong enough for the proper interplay of soul between teacher and child. The child is insufficiently aroused to inner activity. If you observe someone who developed under the influence of a phlegmatic person, and if you follow the course of that person's life into later years, you will often notice a tendency to brain weakness, poor circulation in the brain, or a dulling of brain activity.

And now let us look at the effects of sanguine people on the child—those who allow their sanguine nature to get out of hand. Such an individual responds strongly to every impression, but impressions pass quickly. There is a kind of inner life, but the person's own nature is taken right out into the surroundings. Children cannot keep up with such a teacher, who rushes from one impression to the next, and fails to stimulate the child properly. In order to arouse sufficient inner activity in a child, the teacher must lovingly hold that child to one impression for a certain period of time. If we observe a child who has grown up under the influence of an uncontrolled sanguine nature, we see in later life that there is a certain lack of vital force—an adult life that lacks strength and content.

Thus, if we have the ability to see it (and education depends on a capacity for subtle perception), we recognize various types of people in their fortieth or fiftieth year of life, and we are able to say whether a person has been influenced by the temperament of an educator who was melancholic, phlegmatic, choleric, or sanguine.

The Lasting Effects of a Teacher's Actions

I mention these things in introducing my lectures, not to give instructions on how to work out these things for training teachers, but to show you how actions meant to affect the child's soul life do not just remain in the soul, but go all the way into the physical nature. To educate the soul life of children means to educate them for their whole earthly life, even in their bodily nature.

Anthroposophy is often criticized for wanting to speak of spirit as well as soul. There are many today who become very critical and antagonistic whenever they even hear the word *spirit*, and anthroposophy is easily assumed to be a kind of fantasy. Anthroposophists are accused of reducing the reality of the sense world to a kind of vague abstraction, and those who speak rationally of spiritual things should naturally be unconcerned with such abstraction.

In fact, what anthroposophy attempts in education is to apply the correct principles for bodily education, since we understand that precisely during the first stage of life, the entire physical nature of a child is influenced by soul impulses. Anyone who consciously tries to discover how all physical activity is based fundamentally on soul and spirit can still choose to be a materialist when working on child development between birth and the change of teeth. The way matter works in a child is contained in a unity of soul and spirit. No one can understand matter in a child unless soul and spirit are considered valid. Indeed, soul and spirit are revealed in the outer appearance of matter.

The ability to educate necessitates a sense of responsibility. The considerations I have presented to you strongly arouse one's sense of responsibility as a matter of heartfelt concern. If you take up educational work knowing what affects the young child and that it will continue through all of life as happiness or unhappiness, sickness or health, such knowledge may initially seem like a burden on the soul; but it will also spur you on to develop forces and capacities and above all, as a teacher, a mental attitude that is strong enough to sow "seeds" of soul in the young child that will blossom only later in life, even in old age.

This knowledge of the human being is what anthroposophy presents as the basis for an art of education. It is not merely knowledge of what we find in a human being in a single stage of life—for example, in childhood; it springs from contemplating

all of human earthly life. What, in fact, is a human life on
Earth? When we view a person before us at any given moment,
we may speak of seeing an organism, since each detail is in harmony with the formation of the whole.

To gain insight into the inner connections of size or form in
the individual members of the human organism—how they fit
together, how they harmonize to form both a unity and a multi-
plicity—let us look, for example, at the little finger. Although I
am only looking at the little finger, I also get some idea of the
shape of the earlobe, since the earlobe's form has a certain connection with the form of the little finger, and so on. Both the
smallest and the largest members of the human organism receive
their shape from the whole, and they are also related in form to
every other member. Consequently, we cannot understand, for
example, an organ in the head unless we see it in relation and in
harmony with an organ in the leg or foot. This also applies to
the spatial organism—the organism spread out in space.

Besides having a spatial organism, however, the human being
has also a time organism. We have seen that within the space
organism, the earlobe receives its form from the body as a whole,
as well as from the form of, say, the little finger or knee; but the
time organism must also be considered. The configuration of a
person's soul in the fiftieth year—the person's physical health or
sickness, cheerfulness or depression, clarity or dullness of
mind—is most intimately connected with what was present
there in the tenth, seventh, or fourth year of life. Just as the
members of a spatial organism have a certain relationship to one
another, so do the members of a time organism separated from
one another by time.

From one perspective, it may be asserted that when we are
five years old, everything within us is already in harmony with
what we will be at forty. Of course, a trivial objection may be
raised that one might die young, but it doesn't apply, since other

considerations enter in. Additionally, as a spatial organism, a human being is also organized in time. And if you ever find a finger lying around somewhere, it would have to have been very recently dislodged to look like a finger at all—very soon, it would no longer be a finger. A limb separated from the organism soon shrivels and ceases to be a human limb. A finger separated from the human organism is not a finger at all—it could never live apart from the body, but becomes nothing, and since it cannot exist on its own, it is not real. A finger is real only while united with the whole physical body between birth and death.

Such considerations make it clear that in all our teaching, we must consider the time organism. Imagine what would happen to the space organism if it were treated the way people often treat their time-organism. Let say, for example, that we put some substance into a man's stomach, and it destroys his head. Imagine, however, that we examined only the stomach and never looked at what happened to this substance once it dispersed into the organism, where it eventually reached the head. To understand the human organism, we must be able to examine the process that the substance goes through in the human stomach and also see what it means for the head. In passing from the stomach to the head the substance must continually alter and change; it must be flexible.

In the time organism, we continually sin against children. We teach them to have clear, sharp ideas and become dissatisfied if their ideas are flexible and not sharply defined. Our goal is to teach children in such a way that they retain in their mind what we teach them, so they can tell us just what we told them. We are often especially gratified when a child can reproduce exactly what we taught several years later. But that's like having a pair of shoes made for a child of three and expecting them to fit when the child is ten years old. In reality, our task is to give children living, flexible ideas that can grow in the soul just as the outer physical limbs grow with the body. It is much less trouble to give a child definitions of various things to memorize and retain, but that is like expecting the shoes of a three-year-old to fit a child of ten.

We ourselves must take part in the inner activities of children's souls, and we must consider it a joy to give them something inwardly flexible and elastic. Just as their physical limbs grow, so can their ideas, feelings, impulses, and soon they themselves are able to make something new out of what we gave them. This cannot happen unless we cultivate inner joy in ourselves toward growth and change. We have no use for pedantry or sharply defined ideas of life. We can use only active, life forming forces—forces of growth and increase. Teachers who have a feeling for this growing, creative life have already found their relationship to the children because they contain life within themselves, and such life can then pass on to the children who demand it of them. This is what we need most of all. Much that is dead in our pedagogy and educational systems must be transformed into life. What we need, therefore, is a knowledge of the human being that doesn't say only that a human being is like this or like that. We need knowledge of the human being that affects the whole human being, just as physical nourishment affects the blood. Blood circulates in human beings, and we need human knowledge that gives blood to our souls also; it would not only make us sensible, clever, and intelligent, but also enthusiastic and inwardly flexible, able to enkindle love in us. This would be an art of education that springs from true knowledge of the human being, borne by love.

These have been the introductory remarks I wanted to present about the essential ideas that an art of education must get from anthroposophy. In future lectures we will see how the spirit of anthroposophic education can be realized in the practical details of school.

Lecture Two

The Goal of Waldorf Education

You have seen that education must be based on a more intimate knowledge of the human being than is found in natural science, although it is generally assumed that all knowledge must be grounded in natural science. As we have seen, however, natural science cannot come even close to the reality of the human being, and it doesn't help to base our knowledge on it.

The world is permeated by spirit, and true knowledge of the world must be permeated by spirit as well. Anthroposophy can give us spiritual knowledge of the world, and, with it, spiritual knowledge of the human being, and this alone leads to a true art of education. But don't make the mistake (which is easy to do) that those who consider themselves anthroposophists want to establish "anthroposophic" schools that teach anthroposophy as a worldview in the place of other contemporary worldviews, regardless of whether such views are inspired more by intellect or feeling. It is important to understand and reiterate that this is not at all our intention. What we are examining is mainly concerned with matters of method and the practice of teaching. Men and women who adhere to anthroposophy feel—and rightly so—that the knowledge of the human being it provides can establish some truly practical principles for the way we treat children.

At the Waldorf school in Stuttgart we have been able to pursue an art of education based on anthroposophy for many years; and we have always made it clear to the rest of the world that anthroposophy as such was never taught there. Roman Catholic children receive religious instruction from a priest and Protestant children from a Protestant pastor. Only those children whose parents specifically request it receive religion lessons involving a freer religious instruction based on anthroposophy. Thus, our own anthroposophic worldview as such really has no place in the school work itself.

Moreover, I would like to point out that the true aim and object of anthroposophic education is not to establish as many anthroposophic schools as possible. Naturally, some model schools are needed, where the methods are practiced in detail. There is a need crying out in our time for such schools. Our goal, however, is to enable every teacher to bring the fruits of anthroposophy to their work, no matter where they may be teaching or the nature of the subject matter. There is no intention of using anthroposophic pedagogy to start revolutions, even silent ones, in established institutions. Our task, instead, is to point to a way of teaching that springs from our anthroposophic knowledge of humankind.

Understanding the Human Being

As you know, we need to gain a more intimate observation of human beings than is customary today. In fact, there are some areas where people are learning a very exact kind of observation, especially in regard to visual observation—for example, using a telescope to observe the stars, for surveying, and in many other realms of knowledge. It arises from a sense for exact, mathematical observation. Because of the scientific mindset that has ruled for the past three centuries, nowhere in contemporary civilization do we find the kind of intimate observation that sees the fine and delicate changes in the human soul or body organization. Consequently, people have little to say about the important changes that have occurred in the child's whole physical organization, such as those that happen at the change of the teeth, at puberty, and again after the twentieth year. And so, transitions that have great significance in terms of education—such as the period between the change of teeth and puberty—are simply ignored.

These changes are mentioned, it is true, but only as they affect the actual physical body of the child or are expressed in the soul's more superficial dependence on the physical body. This would require much more delicate observations. Anthroposophy begins by viewing the world as an expression of spiritual forces, which is seldom acknowledged today; it provides exercises that train a person's soul to acquire direct insight into the spirit world. There are some whose destiny has not yet brought them to the point of seeing the spiritual facts for themselves, but anthroposophy has such power that merely beginning such exercises in itself helps people to learn a much more delicate and intimate observation of the human being. After all, you must remember that our soul and spirit is the part of us that, as we have seen, descends from a pre-earthly existence and unites with the inherited physical body. And spiritual research depends on this higher, supersensible part of us; we have supersensible eyes and ears—soul organs such as the eyes and ears of our physical body—so that we can arrive at certain perceptions independently of the body.

Cosmic and Human Cycles

Each night while asleep, a person is unconsciously in a condition that is similar to what is needed for spiritual investigation. When falling asleep, the human soul and spirit leave the physical body, and reenter it when the person awakes. While awake, people use their eyes and ears and move their limbs, and the forces for this come from the spirit and soul aspects of the human being. Genuine knowledge of nature—which doesn't exist yet—would also show that while awake, people's physical actions are controlled by soul and spirit, and that sleep is only an interruption of this activity. Here again, the difference is too subtle to be perceived by modern scientific methods—upon which today's education is based, even when directed toward the earliest years of childhood. A sleeping person is completely surrendered to the activities of the organism to which plant and mineral are also subject.

Anthroposophy or Spiritual Science, on the other hand, strive for precision and accuracy, and it would not be true, of course, to say that while asleep a person is a plant. In a human being, mineral and plant substances have been raised to the level of animal and human. The human organization is not like that of a plant, since a plant has no muscles and nerves, and the human of course has both muscles and nerves, even while asleep. The important thing, however, is very simple; the vegetative function of the plant has nothing to do with nerves and muscles, but it is different for a human being. Activity in a person is related to muscles and nerves, and thus transcends the physical; even human sleep activity is not merely vegetative. (In a certain sense this applies also to animals, but we cannot address this matter now.) Although we find the same impulses in the plant as in the sleeping human being, nevertheless something different happens in a sleeping person.

It may help us to form an idea of this process if we think of it this way: when we are awake, the soul and spirit are integrated with the human organism. The soul and spirit, in turn, have a certain similarity to the cosmos, the whole universe— but keep in mind that it is only a similarity. And careful observation of plant development will show us that in spring, when the snow has melted, we see plants spring out of the earth and unfold their being. Until now, plant growth was controlled by the Sun forces within the Earth, or the stored sunshine of the previous year.

In spring the plants are released, so to speak, by these earthly Sun forces and, as they shoot out of the soil, they are received by the outer sunlight and guided through the summer until the seeds become ripe. Plant growth is again given over to the Earth. Throughout the summer, the Sun's forces gradually descend into the Earth to be stored there; thus, the Earth is always permeated by these accumulated sun forces. We need only remember that millions of years ago Sun forces shone on the plants, which then became coal within the Earth; thus, sunlight is in reality now being burned in our stoves. Likewise— though for a much shorter time—the Sun's forces are preserved in the Earth from summer to summer. Throughout the winter, plants absorb the Sun's forces found in the earth, and during summer, the Sun pours its rays upon them right from the cosmos. So there really is a rhythm in the life of plants—earthly sun-forces, cosmic sun-forces, earthly sun-forces, cosmic sun forces, and so on. Plant life swings from one to the other as a pendulum on a clock.

Now let us turn to the human being. When I fall asleep I leave behind in my body everything of a mineral and plant nature, though, as we have seen, the plant nature in the human being—in contrast to an actual plant—is organized so that spirit and soul can dwell within it. What is left behind in sleep is thus wholly surrendered to its own plant-like activity. It begins to blossom and sprout, and when we go to sleep it is really springtime within us. When we awaken, the plant forces are driven back, and it becomes autumn within us. As soul and spirit arise on awakening, autumn enters us.

Viewing things externally, it is often said that waking is like spring and sleeping like autumn. This is not true, however. Genuine spiritual insight into human nature shows us that

during the first moments of sleep, spring life sprouts and blos-
soms in us, and when we awaken autumn sinks into us like the
setting Sun. While awake, when we are using all our faculties of
soul, it is winter within us. Again we see a rhythm, as in plant-
life. In plant growth we distinguish between earthly activity
and the Sun's activity. In the human being, we find essentially
the same activity imitating the plant; falling asleep—summer
activity, awakening—winter activity, and around again to summer activity, winter activity; but here it takes place in only
twenty-four hours. Human beings have condensed a yearly
rhythm into a day and a night.

These rhythms are similar but not identical, because for a
human being the life of the soul and spirit does not have the
same duration as the life of spirit in the realm of nature. A year
is only a day in the life of the spirits who pervade the cosmos
and permeate the whole course of the year, just as the soul and
spirit of human beings direct the course of their day.

As we consider this, we arrive at this hypothesis. (I must
warn you, by the way, that what I am about to say may seem
very strange to you, but I present it as a hypothesis to demonstrate more clearly what I mean. Let us suppose that a woman
falls asleep, and within her is what I have described as summer
activity. Let us suppose that she continues to sleep without
waking up. What will happen then? The plant element within
her—the element not of soul and spirit—would eventually
become the rhythm of the plant realm. It would go from a
daily rhythm to an annual rhythm. Of course, such a rhythm
does not exist in the human being. Thus, if the physical body
were to go on sleeping as described, the person would be
unable to tolerate the resulting yearly rhythm and would die; if
the human body were all plant activity, it would be organized
differently. The physical body would separate from the soul
and spirit, assume a yearly cycle, and take on purely vegetative

qualities. When we view physical death, which leads to the body's destruction, we see that by being born out of the cosmos, the human being passed from a grand cycle to a small cycle. If a human body is on its own and cannot animate the spirit and soul in itself, it is destroyed, since it cannot immediately find its place in the cosmic rhythm.

Therefore, we see that if we can develop a more delicate faculty for observation, we can gain true insight into the essence of human existence. This is why I said that those who have entered the path of spiritual knowledge, though they may not yet have attained spiritual vision for themselves, will nevertheless feel forces stirring within that lead to spiritual insight. And these are the very forces that act as messengers and mediators of all the spirits at work in the cosmos. Spirit is active in the cosmos where we find the beings who guide the life cycle of the year. This is a new realm to us, but when we observe a human being we can see the presence of soul and spirit in all human life, and here we are on familiar ground. For this reason, it is always easier to exercise a fine faculty of perception in regard to the human soul and spiritual qualities than it is to perceive spirit activity itself in the world.

When we think in ordinary life it is as if thinking, or forming mental images, continually escaped us. When we bump into something or feel something with our fingers—a piece of silk or velvet, for example—we immediately perceive that we have encountered that object, and we can feel its shape by touching its surface. Then we know that as human beings, we have connected with our environment. When we think, however, we do not seem to touch objects around us in this way. Once we have thought about something and made it our own, we can say that we have "apprehended," or "grasped" it (*begreifen*). What do we mean by this? If external objects are alien to us—which is generally true for our thinking—then we do not say we have grasped them. If, for example, a piece of chalk is lying there, and I am standing here moving my hand as one does when speaking, one does not say, "I have grasped the chalk." But if I actually take hold of the chalk with my hand, then I can say, "I have grasped it."

In earlier times, people had a better understanding of what thinking really was, and out of such knowledge, words and expressions flowed into the language that expressed the real thing much better than our modern abstractionists realize. If we have had a mental picture of something, we say we have grasped it. This means we have come into contact with the object—we have "seized" it.[1] Today we no longer realize that we can have intimate contact with objects in our environment through the very expressions in our thinking life. For example, there is a word in our language today that conceals its own meaning in a very hypocritical way. We say "concept" [*Begriff* in German, from *begreifen*]. I have a concept. The word *conceive* (to hold or gather) is contained within it [*greifen*, to grasp, or seize]. I have something that I have grasped, or gathered into myself. We have only the word now; the life has gone out of its meaning.[2]

Examples such as these from everyday life demonstrate the aim and purpose of the exercises described as anthroposophic methods of research in my book *How to Know Higher Worlds*, and in the latter half of *An Outline of Esoteric Science*, and in other works.[3] Consider the exercises in mental imagery. Certain thoughts are held in the mind so that concentration on these

---

1. He is playing here on the words *ergreifen* and *erfassen*.
2. Our English word *concept* derives from Latin *concipere*, to take hold of completely.
3. *How to Know Higher Worlds: A Modern Path of Initiation*, Anthroposophic Press, Hudson, NY, 1994; *An Outline of Esoteric Science*, Anthroposophic Press, Hudson, NY, 1997 (previously *An Outline of Occult Science*).

thoughts may strengthen the soul life. These exercises are based neither on superstition nor merely on fantasy, but on clear thinking and deliberation as exact as that used for mathematics. They lead human beings to develop a capacity for thought in a much more vital and active way than that found in the abstract thinking of people today.

Thinking and the Etheric Body

People today are truly dominated by abstraction. When they work all day with their arms and legs, they feel the need to sleep off their fatigue, because they recognize that their real being has been actively moving arms and legs. What they fail to understand, however, is that when we think, our being is just as active. People cannot see that when they think their being actively flows out and takes hold of the objects of their thinking; this is because they do not perceive the lowest supersensible member of the human being, the *etheric body*, living within the physical body, just as the physical body lives within the external world.

The etheric body can in fact be perceived at the moment when—by practicing the exercises I referred to—a person develops the eye of the soul and the ear of the spirit. One can then see how thinking, which is primarily an activity of the etheric body, is really a spiritual "grasping," or spiritual touching, of the objects around us. Once we have condensed and concentrated our thoughts by means of the exercises mentioned, we experience spirit in such a way that we no longer have the abstract feeling, which is so prevalent today, that objects are far from us. We get a true sense of them that arises from practiced, concentrated thinking. Thinking too will then bring fatigue, and especially after using our powers of thought we will want to have our sleep.

The presence of materialistic ideas is not the worst product of this age of materialism in which we live; educators must also consider another aspect. As educators, we may feel somewhat indifferent to the amount of fatigue caused by people's activities; eventually, people return to their senses, and things even out. But the worst thing for an educator is to watch a child go through years of schooling and receive for the soul only nourishment that bears the stamp of natural science—that is, of material things. Of course, this does not apply only to school science classes; all education today, even in the lowest grades, is based on scientific thinking. This is absorbed by children, it grows up with them, and it penetrates the whole physical organization so that in later years it appears as insomnia.

What is the cause of the sleeplessness of our materialistic time? It is due to the fact that if we think only in a materialistic way, the activity of thought—this "grasping" or "handling" of our environment through thought—does not allow the corresponding organs of the etheric body to become tired since it has become too abstract. Here, only the physical body becomes tired; we fall asleep—the physical body falls asleep—but the etheric becomes nervous and restless and cannot sleep. It draws the soul and spirit back into it, and this condition will necessarily develop gradually into an epidemic of insomnia. This is already happening today. Only by considering such matters can we understand what this materialistic time signifies. It is bad enough that people think materialistic, theoretical thoughts; but in itself this is not really that serious. It is even worse that we experience the effects of materialism in our moral life and in our economic life. And the worst thing is that through materialism, all of childhood is ruined to the point that people can no longer come to terms with moral or spiritual impulses at all.

These things must be known by everyone who recognizes the need to transform our teaching and education. The transitions we have mentioned, such as those that occur at the

change of teeth and at puberty, can be understood only
through intimate observation of the human being. We must
learn to see how a person is inwardly active, so that people
experience their etheric just as they feel their physical body;
they must recognize that when they think about any object,
they are really doing in the etheric what is otherwise done in
the physical human body. If I want to know what an object is
like, I feel it, I contact it, and thus gain a knowledge of its surface. This also applies to my etheric body. I "feel" etherically
and supersensibly the object I want to "grasp," what I wish to
conceptualize. The etheric body is just as active as the physical
body, and correct knowledge of human development can
come only from this knowledge and consciousness of the
etheric body's activity.

The Child's Imitative Nature

If we can activate our thinking in this way and, with this
inwardly active thinking, watch a very young child, we see
how every action performed in that child's environment and
every look that expresses some moral impulse (for the moral
quality of a look contains something that passes into the child
as an imponderable force) flows right into the child and continues to work in the breathing and the circulation of the
blood. The clearest and most concrete statement we can come
to regarding a child is this: "A child is an imitative being
through and through." The way a child breathes or digests in
the more delicate and intimate processes of breathing or
digesting reflects the actions of those around the child.

Children are completely surrendered to their environment. In
adults the only parallel to such devotion is found in religion as
expressed through the human soul and spirit. Religion is
expressed in spiritual surrender to the universe. The religious
life unfolds properly when, with our own spirit, we go beyond

ourselves and surrender to a spiritual worldview—we should flow out into a divine worldview. Adult religious life depends on emancipating soul and spirit from the physical body, when a person's soul and spirit are given up to the divine spirit of the world. Children give up their whole being to the environment. In adults, the activities of breathing, digestion, and circulation are within them, cut off from the external world. In children, however, all such activities are still surrendered to their environment, and they are therefore religious by nature. This is the essential feature of a child's life between birth and the change of teeth; the whole being is permeated with a natural religious element, so to speak, and even the physical body maintains a religious mood.

But children are not surrounded only by beneficial forces that inspire religious devotion in later life. There are also spiritual forces that are harmful, which come from people around children and from other spiritual forces in the world. In this way, this natural religious element in a child's physical body may also be exposed to evil in the environment—children can encounter evil forces. And when I say that even a small child's physical body has a religious quality, I do not mean that children cannot be little demons! Many children are little demons, because they have been open to evil spiritual forces around them.

Our task is to overcome and drive out such forces by applying methods appropriate to our time. As long as a child is an imitative religious being, admonitions do no good. Words can be listened to only when the soul is emancipated to some extent, when its attention can be self-directed. Disapproving words cannot help us deal with a small child. But what we ourselves do in the presence of the child does help, because when a child sees this it flows right in and becomes sense perception. Our actions, however, must contain a moral quality.

If, for example, a man who is color-blind looks at a colored surface, he may see only gray. An adult looks at another person's actions also in this way, seeing only the speed and flow of the gestures. We see the physical qualities but no longer see the moral qualities of the person's actions. A child, on the other hand, sees the moral element, even if only unconsciously, and we must make sure that while in the presence of children, we not only never act in a way that should not be imitated, but never think thoughts that should not enter their souls. Such education of the thoughts is most important for the first seven years of life, and we must not allow ourselves to think any impure, ugly, or angry thoughts when in the company of little children. You may say, "But I can think what I like without altering my outer actions in the least; so the child sees nothing and cannot be influenced by what cannot be seen." Here it is interesting to consider those very peculiar and rather stupid shows given at one time, with so-called thinking horses—horses that could count, and other animals performing tricks demonstrating "intelligence." These things were interesting, though not in the way that most people believed.

I once saw the Elberfeld horses. (I want to speak only of my own observation). I saw the horse belonging to Mr. von Osten, and I could see how he gave answers to his master. Von Osten gave him arithmatic problems to do—not very complicated, it is true, but difficult enough for a horse. The horse had to add and subtract and would give the correct answers by stamping his hoof. Now you can look at this either from the perspective of a modern scientist—for example, the professor who wrote a whole fat book on the horse—or you can view it from an anthroposophic standpoint. The professor began by repudiating all nonprofessional opinions on the matter. (Please do not think that I intend to say anything against natural science, because I am well aware of its value.) In the end, the professor concluded that the horse was able to perceive very delicate movements made by the man—a slight twitch of an eyelid, the most delicate vibrations of certain muscles, and so on. From this, the horse eventually learned what answers corresponded to certain vibrations, and could give the required number of stamps with his hoof. This hypothesis is very clever and intelligent. He then arrives at the inevitable question of whether these things have actually been observed. He asks this question himself, since people are indeed learning to be very conscientious in their research. He answers it, however, by saying that the human senses are not organized in such a way that they perceive such fine delicate movements and vibrations, but a horse can see them. In fact, all he proves is that a horse can see more in a person than a professor can.

But for me, there was something else important—the horse could give the correct answers only when Mr. von Osten stood beside him and spoke. While he talked he kept taking lumps of sugar and placing them in the horse's mouth. The horse was permeated by a taste of sweetness all the time. This is the important thing; the horse felt suffused with sweetness. In such a condition, even a horse can experience things that would otherwise not be possible. In fact, I would put it this way: Mr. von Osten himself constantly lived in the "sweetened horse," the etheric horse that had permeated the physical horse. His thoughts were alive and diffused there, just as they were in his own body; his thoughts lived on in the horse. It was not because a horse has a finer perception than a professor, but because it is not yet as highly organized and thus more susceptible to external influences while its physical body continually absorbs the sweetness.

Indeed, there are such influences that pass from person to person, aroused by things almost—if not wholly—imperceptible to contemporary human beings. Such things occur in the interactions between humankind and animals, and they also occur very much when the soul and spirit are not yet free of the body—that is, during early childhood. Small children can actually perceive the morality behind every look and gesture of those around them, even though this may be no longer possible for those who are older. It is therefore of the greatest importance that we never allow ourselves to think ugly thoughts around children; not only does this live on in their souls, but works right down into the physical body.

There is no question that much is being accomplished these days in many medical or other dissertations, and they reflect the current state of scientific knowledge. But a time will come when there will be something very new in this area. Let me give you a specific example to demonstrate what I mean. A time will come when a person may write a doctoral thesis showing that a disease, perhaps during the forty-eighth year of a person's life, can be traced back to certain evil thoughts in the environment of that person as a child of four or five. This way of thinking can bring us to a genuine understanding of human beings and the capacity for seeing the totality of human life.

We thus have to learn gradually that it is not so much a question of *inventing* from our own abstract thoughts all kinds of things for little children to do, such as using rods and so on. Children do not spontaneously do things like that. Their own soul forces must be aroused, and then they will imitate what the adults do. A little girl plays with a doll because she sees her mother nursing the baby. Whatever we see in adults is present in children as their tendency to imitate. This tendency must be considered in educating children up to the seventh year.

We must bear in mind, however, that what we educate is subject to change in the child's organism; in children everything is done in a more living and animated way than in adults, because children are still a unity of body, soul, and spirit. In adults, the body has been freed from the soul and spirit, and the soul and spirit from the body. Body, soul, and spirit exist side by side as individual entities; in the child they are still firmly united. This unity even penetrates the thinking.

We can see these things very clearly through an example. A small child is often given a so-called "beautiful" doll—a painted creature with glass eyes, made to look exactly like a human being. These little horrors are made to open and shut their eyes and do all sorts of other things. These are then presented to children as "beautiful" dolls. Even from an artistic perspective they are hideous; but I will not enlarge on that now. But consider what really happens to a child who is presented with a doll of this kind, a doll that can open its eyes and so on. At first the child will love it because it is a novelty, but that does not last.

Now, compare that with what happens to a child if I just take a piece of rag and make a doll out of that. Tie it together for a head, make two dots for eyes, and perhaps a big nose, and there you have it. Give that to a child and the rest of that doll will be filled out by the child through imagination in soul and spirit, which are so closely connected with the body. Then, every time that child plays with the doll, there is an inner awakening that remains inwardly active and alive. By making such experiments yourself, you will see what a difference there is between giving a child playthings that leave as much as possible to the power of imagination and giving finished toys that leave nothing for the child's own inner activity. Handwork for small children should only indicate, leaving much for the child's own imagination to do. Working in set forms that can easily be left as they are does not awaken any inner activity in the child, because the imagination cannot get past what is open to the senses.

Physical and Psychical Effects

This shows us what kind of teachers and educators we should be if we really want to approach children in the right way. We need an art of teaching based on a knowledge of human beings—knowledge of the child. This art of education will arise when we find a doctor's thesis that works with a case of diabetes at the age of forty by tracing it back to the harmful effects of the wrong kind of play in the third or fourth year. People will see then what we mean by saying that the human being consists of body, soul, and spirit, and that in the child, body, soul, and spirit are still a unity. The spirit and soul later become freed of the body, and a trinity is formed. In the adult, body, soul, and spirit are pushed apart, as it were, and only the body retains what was absorbed by the individual during early development as the seed of later life.

Now this is the strange thing: when an experience affects the soul, its consequences are soon visible, even when the experience was unconscious; physical consequences, however, take seven or eight times longer to manifest. If you educate a child of three or four so that you present what will influence the soul's life, then the effect of this will appear in the eighth year; and people are usually careful to avoid doing anything with a child of four or five that may affect the soul life in an unhealthy way during the eighth or ninth year. Effects on the physical body take much longer to manifest, because the physical body must free itself of the soul and spirit. Therefore, something that influences the soul life at four or five may come to fruition in the physical body when that person is seven or eight times as old—for example, in the thirty-fifth year. Thus, a person may develop an illness during the late thirties or early forties caused by ill influences that affected that soul while at play as a child of three or four.

If you wish to understand the whole human being, you must also realize that the freeing of the body from soul and spirit in the adult, as opposed to a child's unity of body, soul, and spirit, is not merely abstract theory, but a matter of very specific knowledge, for we are speaking of very different calendars. The time that the body requires to work something out is increasingly lengthened compared to the time needed by the soul. The physical body works more slowly, and harmful influences manifest much later there than in the soul.

Thus, we often see that when we transgress against a little child in the very early years, many things turn out wrong in the teenager's soul-life. This can be corrected, however. It is not very difficult to find ways of helping even seemingly unmanageable children during their teens. They may even become very good and respectable, if somewhat boring, citizens later on. This is not very serious. But the body develops more and more slowly as life goes on, and in the end, long after all the soul difficulties of early youth have been overcome, the physical effects will gradually emerge, and in later life the person will have to contend with arthritis or some other illness.

Real, experiential knowledge of the human being is of the greatest importance. Truly concrete knowledge of the human being, with the power of seeing right into the person, is the only possible basis for a true art of education—an art of education whereby persons may find their place in life and, subject to the laws of their own destinies, fully develop all their powers. Education should never work against a person's destiny, but should help people achieve the fullest possible development of their own predispositions. Often today, people's education lags far behind the talents and tendencies that destiny implanted in them. We must keep pace with these forces to the extent that the human beings in our care can attain all that their destinies will allow—the fullest clarity of thought, the most loving deepening of feeling, and the greatest possible energy and capacity of will.

This can be done only through an art of education and teaching based on a real knowledge of the human being. We will speak more of this in the next lectures.

Lecture Three

In the preceding lectures I have repeatedly spoken of how important it is that teachers turn their attention in particular toward the drastic changes, or metamorphoses, that occur during a child's life—for example, the change of teeth and puberty. We have not fully developed our observation of such changes, because we are used to noticing only the more obvious outer expressions of human nature according to so-called natural laws. What concerns the teacher, however, arises in reality from the innermost center of a child's being, and what a teacher can do for the child affects a child's very inner nature. Consequently, we must pay particular attention to the fact that, for example, at this significant change of teeth, the soul itself goes through a transformation.

Memory Prior to the Change of Teeth

Let us examine a single aspect of this soul-life—the memory, or capacity for remembering. A child's memory is very different before and after the change of teeth. The transitions and developments in human life occur slowly and gradually, so to speak of the change of teeth as a single fixed event in time is only approximate. Nevertheless, this point in time manifests in the middle of the child's development, and we must consider very intensively what takes place at that time.

When we observe a very young child, we find that the capacity to remember has the quality of a soul habit. When a child recalls something during that first period of life until the change of teeth, such remembering is a kind of habit or skill. We might say that when, as a child, I acquire a certain accomplishment—let us say, writing—it arises largely from a certain suppleness of my physical constitution, a suppleness that I have gradually acquired. When you watch a small child taking hold something, you have found a good illustration of the concept of habit. A child gradually discovers how to move the limbs this way or that way, and this becomes habit and skill. Out of a child's imitative actions, the soul develops skillfulness, which permeates the child's finer and more delicate organizations. A child will imitate something one day, then do the same thing again the next day and the next; this activity is performed outwardly, but also—and importantly—within the innermost parts of the physical body. This forms the basis for memory in the early years.

After the change of teeth, the memory is very different, because by then, as I have said, spirit and soul are freed from the body, and picture content can arise that relates to what was experienced in the soul—a formation of images unrelated to bodily nature. Every time we meet the same thing or process, whether due to something outer or inner, the same picture is recalled. The small child does not yet produce these inward pictures. No image emerges for that child when remembering something. When an older child has a thought or idea about some past experience, it arises again as a remembered thought, a thought "made inward." Prior to the age of seven, children live in their habits, which are not inwardly visualized in this way. This is significant for all of human life after the change of teeth.

When we observe human development through the kind of inner vision I have mentioned—with the soul's eyes and ears— we will see that human beings do not consist of only a physical body that can be seen with the eyes and touched with the hands. There are also supersensible members of this being. I have already pointed out the first so-called supersensible human being living within the physical body—the etheric human being. There is also a third member of human nature. Do not be put off by names; after all, we do need to have some terminology. This third member is the *astral body*, which develops the capacity of feeling.

Plants have an etheric body; animals have an astral body in common with humans, and they have feeling and sensation. The human being, who exists uniquely as the crown of earthly creation, has yet a fourth member—the *I-being*. These four members are entirely different from one another, but since they interact with one another they are not generally distinguished by ordinary observation; the ordinary observer never goes far enough to recognize the manifestations of human nature in the etheric body, the astral body, or I-being. We cannot really aspire to teach and educate, however, without knowing these things. One hesitates to say this, because it may be regarded as fantastic and absurd within the broader arena of modern society. It is nevertheless the truth, and an unbiased knowledge of the human being will not disagree.

The way that the human being works through the etheric body, astral body, and I-being is unique and is significant for educators. As you know, we are used to learning about the physical body by observing it—living or dead—and by using the intellect connected with the brain to elucidate what we have thus perceived with the senses. This type of observation alone, however, will never reveal anything of the higher members of human nature. They are inaccessible to methods of observation based only on sense-perception and intellectual activity. If we think only in terms of natural laws, we will never understand the etheric body, for example. Therefore, new methods should be introduced into colleges and universities.

Observation through the senses and working in the intellect of the brain enable us to observe only the physical body. A very different training is needed to enable a person to perceive, for example, how the etheric body manifests in the human being. This is really necessary, not just for teachers of every subject, but even more so for doctors.

The Etheric Body and the Art of Sculpting

First, we should learn to sculpt and work with clay, as a sculptor works, modeling forms from within outward, creating forms out of their own inner principles, and guided by the unfolding of our own human nature. The form of a muscle or bone can never be comprehended by the methods of contemporary anatomy and physiology. Only a genuine sense of form reveals the true forms of the human body. But when we say such things we will immediately be considered somewhat crazy. But Copernicus was considered a bit mad in his time; even as late as 1828 some leaders of the Church considered Copernican theories insane and denied the faithful any belief in them!

Now let's look at the physical body; it is heavy with mass and subject to the laws of gravity. The etheric body is not subject to gravity—on the contrary, it is always trying to get away. Its tendency is to disperse and scatter into far cosmic spaces. This is in fact what happens right after death. Our first experience after death is the dispersal of the etheric body. The dead physical body follows the laws of Earth when lowered into the grave; or when cremated, it burns according to physical laws just like any other physical body. This is not true of the etheric body, which works away from Earth, just as the physical body strives toward Earth. The etheric body, however, does not necessarily extend equally in all directions, nor does it strive away from Earth in a uniform way. Now we arrive at something that might seem very strange to you; but it can in fact be perceived by the kind of observation I have mentioned.

When you look up into the heavens, you see that the stars are clustered into definite groups, and that these groups are all different from one another. Those groups of stars attract the etheric human body, drawing it out into the far spaces. Let's imagine someone here in the center.

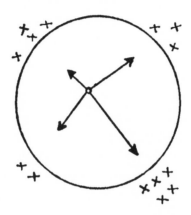

The different groups of stars are drawing out the etheric body in varying degrees; there is a much stronger attraction from one group of stars than from another, thus the etheric body is not drawn out equally on all sides but to varying degrees in the different directions of space. Consequently, the etheric body is not spherical, but, through this dispersion of the etheric, certain definite forms may arise in the human being through the cosmic forces that work down from the stars. These forms remain in us as long as we live on Earth and have an etheric body within us.

If, for example, we take the upper part of the thigh, we see that both the form of the muscle and the form of the bone are shaped by influences from the stars. We need to discover how these very different forms can arise from different directions of cosmic space. We must try to model these varying forms in clay, and we will find that, in one particular form, cosmic forces act to produce length; in another the form is rounded off more quickly. Examples of the latter are the round bones, and the former are the more tubular bones.

Like sculptors, therefore, we must develop a feeling for the world—the kind of feeling that, in ancient humankind, was present as a kind of instinctive consciousness. It was clearly expressed in the Eastern cultures of prehistory, thousands of years before our era; but we still find it in Greek culture. Just consider how contemporary, materialistic artists are often baffled by the forms of the Greek sculptors. They are baffled, because they believe the Greeks worked from models, which they examined from all sides. But the Greeks still had a feeling that the human being is born from the cosmos, and that the cosmos itself forms the human being. When the Greeks created their Venus de Milo (which causes contemporary sculptors to despair), they took what flowed from the cosmos; and although this could reveal itself only imperfectly in any earthly work, they tried to express it in the human form they were creating as much as possible. The point is that, if you really attempt to mold the human form according to nature, you cannot possibly do it by slavishly following a model, which is the contemporary studio method. One must be able to turn to the great "cosmic sculptor," who forms the human being from a *feeling for space*, which a person can also acquire.

This then is the first thing we must develop. People think they can gauge the human form by drawing a line going through vertically, another through the outstretched arms and another front to back; there you have the three dimensions. But in doing this, they are slaves to the three dimensions of space, and this is pure abstraction. If you draw even a single line through a person in the right way, you can see that it is subject to manifold forces of attraction—this way or that, in every direction of space. This "space" of geometry, about which Kant produced such unhappy definitions and spun out such abstract theories—this space itself is in fact an organism, producing varied forces in all directions.

Human beings are likely to develop only the grosser physical senses, and do not inwardly unfold this fine delicate feeling for space experienced in all directions. If we could only allow this feeling for space to take over, the true image of the human being would arise. Out of an active inner feeling, you will see the plastic form of the human being emerge. If we develop a feeling for handling soft clay, we have the proper conditions for understanding the etheric body, just as the activity of human intellect connected with the brain provides the appropriate conditions for understanding the physical body.

We must first create a new method of acquiring knowledge—a kind of plastic perception together with an inner plastic activity. Without this, knowledge stops short at the physical body, since we can know the etheric body only through *images,* not through ideas. We can really understand these etheric images only when we are able to reshape them ourselves in some way, in imitation of the cosmic shaping.

The Astral Body in Relation to Music

Now we can move on to the next member of the human being. Where do things stand today in regard to this? On the one hand, in modern life the advocates of natural science have become the authorities on the human being; on the other hand we find isolated, eccentric anthroposophists, who insist that there are also etheric and astral bodies, and when they describe the etheric and astral bodies, people try to understand those descriptions with the kind of thinking applied to understanding the physical body, which doesn't work. True, the astral body expresses itself in the physical body, and its physical expression can be comprehended according to the laws of natural science.

However, the astral body itself, in its true inner being and function, cannot be understood by those laws. It can be understood only by understanding music—not just externally, but inwardly. Such understanding existed in the ancient East and still existed in a modified form in Greek culture. In modern times it has disappeared altogether. Just as the etheric body acts through cosmic shaping, the astral body acts through cosmic music, or cosmic melodies. The only earthly thing about the astral body is the beat, or musical measure. Rhythm and melody come directly from the cosmos, and the astral body consists of rhythm and melody.[1]

It does no good to approach the astral body with what we understand as the laws of natural science. We must approach it with what we have acquired as an inner understanding of music. For example, you will find that when the interval of a third is played, it can be felt and experienced within our inner nature. You may have a major and minor third, and this division of the scale can arouse considerable variations in the feeling life of a person; this interval is still something inward in us. When we come to the fifth interval, we experience it at the surface, on our boundary; in hearing the fifth, it is as though we were only just inside ourselves. We feel the sixth and seventh intervals to be finding their way outside us. With the fifth we are passing beyond ourselves; and as we enter the sixth and the seventh, we experience them as external, whereas the third is completely internal. This is the work of the astral body—the

---

1. See Rudolf Steiner, *The Inner Nature of Music and the Experience of Tone*, Anthroposophic Press, Hudson, NY, 1983; also Armin Husemann, *The Harmony of the Human Body: Musical Principles in Human Physiology*, Floris Books, Edinburgh, 1994.

musician in every human being—which echoes the music of the cosmos. All this is at work in the human being and finds expression in the physical human form. If we can really get close to such a thought in trying to comprehend the world, it can be an astonishing experience for us.

You see, we are speaking now of something that can be studied very objectively—something that flows from the astral body into the human form. In this case, it is not something that arises from cosmic shaping, but from the musical impulse streaming into the human being through the astral body. Again, we must begin with an understanding of music, just as a sculptural understanding is necessary in understanding the etheric body's activities. If you take the part of the human being that goes from the shoulderblades to the arms, that is the work of the tonic, the keynote, living in the human being. In the upper arm, we find the interval of the second. (You can experience all this in eurythmy.) And in the lower arm the third—major and minor. When you come to the third, you find two bones in the lower arm, and so on, right down into the fingers.

This may sound like mere words and phrases, but through genuine observation of the human being, based on spiritual science, we can see these things with the same precision that a mathematician uses in approaching mathematical problems. We cannot arrive at this through any kind of mystical nonsense: it must be investigated with precision. In order that students of medicine and education really comprehend these things, their college training must be based on an inner understanding of music. Such understanding, permeated with clear, conscious thinking, leads back to the musical understanding of the ancient East, even before Greek culture began. Eastern architecture can be understood only when we understand it as religious perception descended into form.

Just as music is expressed only though the phenomenon of time, architecture is expressed in space. The human astral and etheric bodies must be understood in the same contrasting way. We can never explain the life of feeling and passion with natural laws and so-called psychological methods. We can understand it only when we consider the human being as a whole in terms of music. A time will come when psychologists will not describe a diseased condition of the soul life as they do today, but will speak of it in terms of music, as one would speak, for example, of a piano that is out of tune.

Please do not think that anthroposophy is unaware of how difficult it is to present such a view in our time. I understand very well that many people will consider what I have presented as pure fantasy, if not somewhat crazy. But, unfortunately, a so-called "reasonable" way of thinking can never portray the human being in actuality. We must develop a new and expanded rationality for these matters. In this connection, it is extraordinary how people view anthroposophy today. They cannot imagine that anything exists that transcends their powers of comprehension, but that those same powers can in fact eventually reach.

Recently, I read a very interesting book by Maeterlinck translated into German. There was a chapter about me, and it ended in an extraordinary and very amusing way. He says: "If you read Steiner's books you will find that the early chapters are logically correct, intelligently thought-out and presented in a perfectly scientific form. But as you read on, you get the impression that the author has gone mad." Maeterlinck, of course, has a perfect right to his opinions. Why should he not have the impression that the writer was a clever man when he wrote the first part of the book, but went mad when he wrote the later part? But simply consider the actual situation. Maeterlinck believes that in the first chapters of these books the author was clever, but in the last chapters he had gone mad. So we get the extraordinary fact that this man writes several books, one after the other. Consequently, in each of these books the first few chapters make him seem very smart, but in later chapters he seems mad, then clever again, then mad, and so on. You see how ridiculous it is when one has such a false picture. When writers—otherwise deservedly famous—write in such a way, people fail to notice what nonsense it is. This shows how hard it is, even for such an enlightened person as Maeterlinck, to reach reality. On the firm basis of anthroposophy we have to speak of a reality that is considered unreal today.

I-being and the Genius of Language

Now we come to the I-being. Just as the astral body can be investigated through music, the true nature of the I-being can be studied through the word. It may be assumed that everyone, even doctors and teachers, accepts today's form of language as a finished product. If this is their standpoint, they can never understand the inner structure of language. This can be understood only when you consider language, not as the product of our modern mechanism, but as the result of the *genius* of language, working vitally and spiritually. You can do this when you attempt to understand the way a word is formed.[2]

There is untold wisdom in words, way beyond human understanding. All human characteristics are expressed in the way various cultures form their words, and the peculiarities of any nation may be recognized in their language. For example, consider the German word *Kopf* ("head"). This was originally connected with the rounded form of the head, which you also find

2. See Rudolf Steiner, *The Genius of Language: Observations for Teachers*, Anthroposophic Press, Hudson, NY, 1995.

in the word *Kohl* ("cabbage"), and in the expression *Kohlkopf* ("head of cabbage"). This particular word arises from a feeling for the form of the head. You see, here the I has a very different concept of the head from what we find in *testa*, for example, the word for "head" in the Romance languages, which comes from *testifying*, or "to bear witness." Consequently, in these two instances, the feelings from which the words are formed come from very different sources.

If you understand language in this inward way, then you will see how the I-organization works. There are some districts where lightning is not called *Blitz* but *Himmlitzer*. This is because the people there do not think of the single flashes of lightning so much as the snakelike form. People who say *Blitz* picture the single flash and those who say *Himmlitzer* picture the zig-zag form. This then is how humans really live in language as far as their I is concerned, although in the current civilization, they have lost connection with their language, which has consequently become something abstract. I do not mean to say that if you have this understanding of language you will already have attained inward clairvoyant consciousness, whereby you will be able to behold beings like the human I. But you will be on the way to such a perception if you accompany your speaking with inner understanding.

Thus, education in medical and teacher training colleges should be advanced as indicated, so that the students' training may arouse in them an inner feeling for space, an inner relationship to music, and an inner understanding of language. Now you may argue that the lecture halls are already becoming empty and, ultimately, teacher training colleges will be just as empty if we establish what we've been speaking of. Where would all this lead to? Medical training keeps getting longer and longer. If we continue with our current methods, people will be sixty by the time they are qualified!

The situation we are speaking of is not due in any way to inner necessity but is related to the fact that inner conditions are not being fulfilled. If we fail to go from abstractions to plastic and musical concepts and to an understanding of the cosmic word—if we stop short at abstract ideas—our horizon will be endless; we will continue on and on and never come to a boundary, to a point where we can survey the whole. The understanding that will come from understanding sculpting and music will make human beings more rational—and, believe me, their training will actually be accelerated rather than delayed. Consequently, this inner course of development will be the correct method of training educators, and not only teachers, but those others who have so much to contribute to educational work—the doctors.

The Therapeutic Nature of Teaching

Given what I spoke of in the introductory lectures concerning the relationship between educational methods and the physical health of children, it should be clear to you that real education cannot be developed without considering medicine. Teachers should be able to assess various conditions of health or disease among their children. Otherwise, a situation will arise that is already being felt—that is, a need for doctors in the schools. The doctor is brought in from outside, which is the worst possible method we could adopt. How do such doctors stand in relation to the children? They do not know the children, nor do they know, for example, what mistakes the teachers have made with them, and so on. The only way is to cultivate an art of education that contains so much therapy that the teacher can continually see whether the methods are having a good or bad influence on the children's health. Reform is not accomplished by bringing doctors into the schools from outside, no matter how necessary this may seem to be. In any case, the kind of training doctors get these days does not prepare them for what they must do when they are sent into the schools.[3]

In aiming at an art of education we must provide a training based on knowledge of the human being. I hesitate to say these things because they are so difficult to comprehend. But it is an error to believe that the ideas of natural science can give us full understanding of the human being, and an awareness of that error is vital to the progress of the art of education. Only when we view children from this perspective do we see, for example, the radical and far-reaching changes that occur with the coming of the second teeth, when the memory becomes a pictorial memory, no longer related to the physical body but to the etheric body. In actuality, what is it that causes the second teeth? It is the fact that, until this time, the etheric is almost completely connected with the physical body; and when the first teeth are forced out, something separates from the physical body. If this were not the case, we would get new teeth every seven years. (Since people's teeth decay so quickly nowadays, this might seem to be a good thing, and dentists would have to find another job!) When the etheric body is separated, what formerly worked in the physical body now works in the soul realm.

If you can perceive these things and can examine the children's mouths without their knowledge, you will see for yourself that this is true. It is always better when children do not know they are being observed. Experimental psychology so often fails because children are aware of what is being done.

You can examine a child's second teeth and find that they have been formed by the etheric body into a modeled image of

---

3. Steiner is referring to doctors with no knowledge of the Waldorf methods of education.

the memory; and the shape of the teeth created by the etheric will indicate how the memory of the child will develop. Except for slight alterations in position here or there, you cannot physically change the second teeth once they are through—unless you are able to go so far as, for example, the dentist Professor Romer. He has written a book on dentistry—a new art of medicine based on anthroposophic principles—where he speaks of certain changes that can be effected even after the second teeth are established. But this need not concern us further.

When the etheric body is loosened and exists on its own after the change of teeth, the building of memory leaves the physical realm and remains almost entirely in the element of soul; indeed, this fact can put teachers on the right track. Before this change, the soul and spirit formed a unity with the physical and etheric. After this, the physical—previously acting in conjunction with the soul—is expressed as the second teeth, and what collaborated with the physical in this process separates and manifests as an increased power to form ideas and as the formation and reliability of memory.

Once you have acquired such insight into human nature, you will discover much that will help in your teaching. You must permeate yourselves with this spiritual knowledge of the human being and enliven it in yourselves; your observations of children will then inspire you with ideas and methods for teaching, and this inner inspiration and enthusiasm will penetrate your practical work. The rules established in introductory texts on education produce only abstract activity in the soul. But what arises from anthroposophic knowledge penetrates the will and the efforts of teachers; it becomes the impulse for everything done in the classroom.

A living knowledge of the human being brings life and order to the soul of a teacher. But if teachers study only teaching methods that arise from natural science, they may get some clever ideas of what to do with the children, but they will be unable to carry them out. A teacher's skill and practical handling of children must arise from the living spirit within, and this is where purely scientific ideas have no place. If teachers can acquire a true knowledge of the human being, they will become aware of how, when the etheric body is freed at the change of teeth, the child has an inner urge to receive everything in the form of images. The child's own inner being wants to become "image." During the first stage of life, impressions lack this picture-forming tendency; they are transformed instead into habits and skills in the child; memory itself *is* habit and skill.

Children want to imitate, through the movement of the limbs, everything they see happening around them; they have no desire to form any inner images. But after the change of teeth, you will notice how children come to know things very differently. Now they want to experience pictures arising in the soul; consequently, teachers must bring everything into a pictorial element in their lessons. Creating images is the most important thing for teachers to understand.

Teaching Writing and Reading

When we begin to view the facts, however, we are immediately faced with certain contradictions. Children must learn to read and write, and when they come to school we assume they will first learn to read, and after that they will learn to write in connection with their reading. Let's consider, however, the reality of letters—what it means when we take a pen to paper and try to express through writing what is in the mind. What is the relationship between the printed letters of today and the original picture-language of ancient times? How were we taught these things? We show children a capital *A* and a lowercase *a*, but what in the world do these letters have to do with the sound "ah"? There is no relationship at all between the form of the letter *A* and the sound "ah."

When the art of writing arose, things were different. In certain areas, pictorial signs were used, and a kind of pictorial painting was employed. Later, this was standardized; but originally those drawings copied the process and feeling of the sounds; thus, what appeared on paper was, to some extent, a reproduction of what lived in the soul. Modern characters, however, are alien to a small child's nature, and it is little wonder that when certain early peoples first saw printed letters, it had a peculiar effect on them. When the people of Europe came among the Native Americans and showed them how they expressed their thoughts on paper, the Native Americans were alarmed and considered it the work of the devil; they were afraid of the little demons lurking behind those written letters. They immediately concluded that the Europeans engaged in black magic, since people have a habit of attributing to black magic whatever they cannot understand.

But what is the truth of the matter? We know that when we utter the sound "ah," we express wonder and admiration. Now, it is very natural to try to reproduce this sound with the whole body and express it in a gesture of the arms. If you copy this gesture (stretching the arms obliquely above the head) you get the capital *A*. When you teach writing, you can, for example, begin with a feeling of wonder, and proceed with the children to some kind of painting and drawing, and in this way you can bring their inner and outer experiences into that painting and drawing.

Consider another example. I tell a girl to think of a fish and ask her to paint it (awkward though this may be). It must be done in a particular way, not simply as she might prefer, but with the head of the fish in front, like this, and the rest of the fish here. The child paints the fish, and thus, through a kind of painting and drawing, she produces a written character. You then tell her to pronounce the word *fish*—"fish." Now take away the *ish*, and from *fish* you have arrived at her first written letter, *f.*

In this way a child will come to understand how pictorial writing arose, and how it developed into contemporary writing. The forms were copied, but the pictures were abandoned. This is how drawing the various sounds arose. You do not need to make a special study of how such things evolved. This is not really necessary for teachers, since they can develop them out of their own intuition and power to think. Have a boy, for example, paint the upper lip of a mouth, and then pronounce the word *mouth*. Leave out the *outh*, and you get the *m*. In this way you can relate all the written characters to some reality, and the child will constantly develop a living, inner activity.

Thus, you should teach the children writing first, and let today's abstract letters arise from tangible reality; when a child learns to write in this way, the whole being is engaged in the process. Whereas, if you begin with reading, then only the head organization participates in an abstract way. In writing, the hand must participate as well, and in this way the whole human being is aroused to activity. When you begin with writing—writing developed through the formation of images and drawing forms—your teaching will approach the child's whole being. Then you can move on to teaching reading; and what was developed out of the child's whole being through drawing can be understood by the head. This method of teaching writing and reading will naturally take longer, but it will have a far healthier effect on the whole earthly life from birth to death.

These things can be done when the practical work of the school flows out of a real spiritual knowledge of the human being. Such knowledge can, through its own inner force, become the teaching method in our schools. The desires of those who earnestly seek a new art of education live in this; but its essence can be truly found only when we are unafraid to look for a full knowledge of the human being in body, soul, and spirit.

Lecture Four

Moral Development after the Change of Teeth

We have been speaking of ways to teach reading and writing according to the needs of the soul and spirit of children. If you can inwardly understand the relationship of soul and spirit to the physical body at the change of teeth, you not only see the truth of what has been said, but you will be also able to work it out in practical details. Until the change of teeth, a human being lives entirely in the senses. A child surrenders entirely to the environment and is thus by nature a religious being.

At the change of teeth, however, the senses, which the permeate a small child's whole being, now come to the surface; they disengage from the rest of the organism and go their separate ways, so to speak. This means that the soul and spirit are freed from the physical body and the child can inwardly develop as an individual. Soul and spirit become independent, but you must bear in mind that the soul and spirit do not really become intellectual until puberty, because the intellect does not assume its natural place in a child's development before then.

Before that time, a child lacks the forces to meet an appeal to the intellect. Between the change of teeth and puberty, the forces of comprehension and the whole activity of soul have a pictorial quality. It is a kind of aesthetic comprehension that may be characterized in this way: until the change of teeth children want to imitate what happens around them, what is done in front of them. Their motor systems are exerted in such a way—both in general and individually—that they enter an inner, loving relationship with all that surrounds them.

This alters at the change of teeth, when the child no longer goes by what is seen, but by what is revealed in the feelings and soul mood of the educator or teacher. The young child's soul before the change of teeth is not yet guided by the authority of a teacher. Naturally, such transitions are gradual rather than sudden; but, typically, a small child pays little attention to the subject or meaning of what is said; a child lives much more in the *sound* of words—in the whole way the speech is formulated. Closer observation shows that when you simply lay down the law and say to a child, "You must not do this," it makes very little impression. But when, with its own conviction, as it were, your mouth says, "Do this," or another time, "Don't do that," there should be a noticeable difference in *how* these words are spoken. The child will notice the difference between saying "You should not do that" with a certain intonation, and "That's right, you may do that." The intonation reveals the activity of speech, which acts as a guide for the very young child.

Children are unconcerned with the meaning of words and, indeed, with any manifestation of the world around them, until after the change of teeth. Even then, it is not yet the intellectual aspect that concerns them, but an element of feeling. They take it in as one takes anything from acknowledged authority. Before puberty, a child cannot intellectually determine right and wrong. People may speculate about these things as much as they like, but direct observation shows what I have said to be true. This is why all moral concepts brought before a child must be pictorial in nature.

The subject being taught and moral training can thus be interwoven. If, for example, you are presenting examples of history—not in a stilted, pedantic way, with all kinds of moral maxims, but with simple feelings of like and dislike—you can show that what is moral is pleasing to you, and what is not moral is displeasing. Thus, during the time between the change of teeth and puberty, a child can acquire sympathy for what is good and antipathy toward what is bad. We do not begin by giving children *commands*, because commands will not have the desired effect. It may be possible to enslave children with commands, but we can never foster the moral life in this way, which instead must spring from the depths of the soul. We can do this only when, quite apart from commanding or forbidding, we are able to arouse a fine feeling for good and bad in the child—a feeling for beautiful and ugly and for true and false.

The teacher respected by the child as an authority should personify what is good, true, and beautiful. A child brought up on precepts can never become fully human, formed and developed from the whole of the child's inner nature. Precepts consider only the development of the head. We can foster the development of the heart—indeed, the whole person—if we can arouse the feeling at that age that something is true, beautiful, or good, because the revered teacher thinks it to be true, beautiful, or good. In a person, in an actual human being, a child will look for manifestations of truth, beauty, and goodness. When the picture of truth, beauty, and goodness comes from the individuality of the educator, it affects the child with the most amazing intensity. The whole being of the child is exerted to find an inner echo of what the teacher says or otherwise makes perceptible. This is most important, therefore, in the educational methods we use for children between seven and fourteen.

Of course, there are obvious objections to such a statement; the idea of "object-lessons," or teaching based on sense-perception, is so misunderstood these days that people believe they should give children only what they can *understand*, and since we live in an era of the intellect, such understanding is intellectual. It is not yet understood that it is possible to understand things with soul forces other than those of the intellect—and recommendations for so-called "object-lessons" can drive one nearly to despair.

It is a terrible mindset that wants to pin the teacher down to the children's level of understanding all the time. If you really set up the principle of giving children only "what they can understand," one cannot gain a concept of what it means for a child of six or seven to have accepted something based on the unquestioned authority of a teacher. Because the teacher thought something was true or beautiful, the child accepted it, and it will accompany that child throughout life. It grows with the child as the child grows. And at thirty or forty years of age—after more mature experiences—that individual may again find what was accepted at eight or nine based on the authority of a beloved teacher. It springs back into the adult's life again, and now it can be understood because of adult experiences.

There is a most wonderful life-giving power, when things already contained within a person's soul emerge and unite with the essence of what was acquired in the meantime. Such life-giving forces can be born in the person only when what was accepted by the child on the authority of the teacher arises in the soul, through the maturity of subsequent experience. If memories are connected only with the intellect, then a child is robbed of life-giving forces. In these matters we must come to perceive the human being in a much more intimate way than is usual today.

Beginning with the Whole in Mathematics

It is essential that we make sure the child is not driven to a one-sided intellectuality. This will nevertheless be the situation if our teaching is permeated with intellectual thought. What I am saying here applies to everything children should be taught between the change of teeth and puberty. It is most important that mathematics, for example, should not be intellectualized; even in mathematics, we should begin with what is real.

Now imagine that I have ten beans here in front of me. This pile of 10 beans is the *reality*—it is a whole—but I can divide it into smaller groups. If I began by saying, "3+3+4 beans = 10 beans," then I am starting with a thought instead of an actuality. Let's do it the other way around and say, "Here are 10 beans. I move them around, and now they are divided into groups—3 here, 3 again here, and another group of 4 that, together, make up the whole."

When I begin this way with the total actually in front of me, and then go on to the numbers to be added together, I am sticking with reality; I proceed from the whole, which is constant, to its parts. The parts can be grouped in various ways—for example, $10 = 2+2+3+3$—but the whole is constant and invariable, and this is the greater reality. Thus, I must teach children to add by proceeding from the whole to the parts. Genuine knowledge of the human being shows us that, at this age, a child will have nothing to do with abstractions, such as addenda, but wants everything concrete; and this requires a reversal of the usual method of teaching mathematics. In teaching addition, we have to proceed from the whole to the parts, showing that it can be divided in various ways. This is the best method to help us awaken forces of observation in children, and it is truly in keeping with their nature. This applies also to the other rules of mathematics. If you say, "What must we take away from 5 in order to leave 2?" you will arouse much more interest in children than if you say, "Take 3 from 5." And the first question is also much closer to real life. These things happen in real life, and in your teaching methods you can awaken a sense of reality in children at this age.

A sense for reality is sorely lacking in our time, and this is because (though not always acknowledged) something is considered true when it can be observed and is logical. But logic alone cannot establish truth, because truth can arise only when something is not only logical but accords with reality. We hear some very strange ideas about this nowadays. For example, Einstein's theory of relativity—which is brilliant and, from certain points of view, significant—presents ideas that, if one has a sense for reality at all, leave one feeling torn and disintegrated. You may recall his watch that travels out into space with the speed of light supposedly unchanged. But you only need to imagine what it would be like when it returned—completely pulverized, to say the least!

Something is placed before you that can be well-reasoned and very logical; the theory of relativity is as logical as can be, but in many of its applications, it does not accord with reality. Such things make a deep impression on people today, because we no longer have a fine feeling for reality. When we consider the needs of children during this second period of life it is most important to give them realities rather than abstractions. This is the only way we can prepare them properly for later life—not just in thinking, but in the forces of feeling and will. We must first recognize the true nature of the child before we can correctly tackle education, whether at school or at home.

The Natural Religious Feeling in Children

Before we become earthly beings, as I have told you before, we are beings of soul and spirit living in a world of soul and spirit. We come to earth and as beings of soul and spirit and unite with the physical and etheric seed; this physical, etheric seed arises partly through the activity of the soul and spirit itself, and partly through the stream of inheritance that passes through the generations, and finally, through the father and mother, approaches the human being who wishes to incarnate in a physical body. If we consider this soul and spirit descending to Earth, we cannot help but view it with reverence and awe. The unfolding of the child's being must fill us as teachers with feelings of reverence—indeed, we could speak of priestly feelings; because, the way soul and spirit are unveiled in the child really does constitute a revelation of that soul and spirit within the physical and etheric realm.

This mood of soul allows us to see the child as a being sent down to Earth by the Gods to incarnate in a physical body. It arouses within us the proper attitude of mind for our work in the school. But we learn to perceive only through true observation of what gradually manifests prior to the change of teeth—by observing the building of a child's body, the ordering of chaotic movements, the "ensouling" of gestures, and so on. We can see in all this, springing from the center of a child's being, the effects of the human being's experiences in the divine spiritual realm before coming to Earth.

Only on the basis of this knowledge can we correctly understand what expresses itself in the life and activities of children under seven. They simply continue in their earthly life a tendency of soul that was the most essential aspect of life before birth. In the spiritual realm, a human being surrenders completely to the spirit all around, lives outside itself, though more individually than on Earth. The human being wants to continue this tendency toward devotion in earthly life—wants to continue in the body the activity of pre-earthly life in the spiritual worlds. This is why the whole life of a small child is naturally religious.

Imagery after the Age of Seven

It is very different when we come to the change of teeth. Now, with their individuality, but on the model delivered by its inheritance, children make their own bodies. At this age, a child acquires for the first time a body formed from the individuality. Human beings come to Earth with a remembered tendency; this then develops into a more pictorial and plastic memory. Therefore, what is produced from the impulses of former earthly lives causes life between the change of teeth and puberty to seem familiar. It is very important for us to realize that a child's experience at this age is like recognizing an acquaintance on the street.

This experience—lowered one level into the subconscious—is what happens in the physical and moral nature of a child at this age. The child experiences what is being learned as old and familiar. The more we can appeal to that feeling, recognizing that we are giving the child old and familiar knowledge, the more pictorial and imaginative we can make our teaching, and the better we will teach, because that individual saw these things as images in the spiritual life and knows that his or her own being rests within those images; they can be understood because they are already well known. The child has not yet developed any clearly defined or individual sympathies and antipathies, but has a general feeling of sympathy or antipathy toward what is found on the Earth, just as I might feel sympathy if I meet a friend or antipathy if I meet someone who once struck me on the head. If we keep in mind that these general feelings are there, and if we work on this hypothesis, our teaching will be on the right track.

The Individual after Puberty

Then a child reaches puberty, and an important change occurs. The more general feelings of sympathy and antipathy give way to individualized feelings. Each thing has or lacks value in the child's eyes, but differently now. This is because at puberty, a human being's true destiny begins to be felt. Before this time, children had more general feelings about life, viewing it as an old acquaintance. Now, having attained sexual maturity, a child feels that the individual experiences that arise are related to destiny. Only when a person views life in terms of destiny does it become one's own individual life in the proper way. Therefore, what we experienced before must be recalled a second time in order to connect it with one's destiny.

Before fourteen, everything must be based on the teacher's authority, but if it is to become a part of a child's destiny it must be presented again after fourteen, to be experienced in an individual way. This must in no way be ignored. With regard to moral concepts, we must bring the child before puberty to have a liking for the good and such a dislike for evil. Then, during the next period of life, things that were developed in sympathy and antipathy appear again in the soul, and the growing individual will make what was loved into precepts for the self, and what was repugnant, the person must now avoid. This is freedom, but as human beings we can find it only if, before we come to "Do this" and "Don't do that," we feel attracted to the good and repelled by the bad. A child must learn morality through feeling.

With regard to religion, we must be clear that young children are naturally religious. At the change of teeth, when the soul and spirit become more free of the body, this close relationship with nature falls away, and thus what was formerly natural religion must be lifted to a religion of the soul. Only after puberty does religious understanding arise, and then, once the spirit has become free, what was formerly expressed in imitation of the father or mother must be surrendered to the invisible, supersensible forces. Thus, what has always been present in the child as a seed gradually develops in a concrete way. Nothing is grafted onto the child; it arises from the child's own being.

True Reform in Education

Here is an extraordinary fact you can verify for yourselves; with all relatively rational people—and nearly everyone is rational these days (and I mean that seriously)—you find that people have been educated only to be rational, only to work with their heads, and no more. To educate the whole person is not as easy. You only have to read what very sensible people have written about education, and you repeatedly encounter this sort of statement: "Nothing should be presented to a child from outside; but what is already there should be developed." You can read that everywhere, but how is it done? That is the question. It is not a matter of establishing principles. Programmatic principles are easy to come by, but what matters is to live in reality. This is what we must aim for, but we will find ourselves nearly overwhelmed by the difficulties and dangers in our path.

Thirty, forty, or a hundred people can sit down together today and draft treatises on the best methods for teaching and education and other recommendations, and I am convinced that in most cases they do it very cleverly. I am not being ironic—our materialistic culture has reached its zenith. Everywhere societies are being established and principles elaborated. In themselves, these are splendid, but they accomplish nothing. That is why the Waldorf school came into being in such a way that there were no set principles or systems—only children and teachers. We have to consider not only the individuality of every single child, but the individuality of every single teacher as well. We must know our teachers. It is easy to draft rules and principles that tell teachers what to do and not do. But what matters is the capacities of individual teachers, and the development of their capacities; they do not need educational precepts, but a knowledge of the human being that takes them into life itself and considers whole persons in a living way. You see, our job must always be *development*, but we must know where to look for what we wish to develop. We must link religious feeling—and later, religious thinking—with imitation during the first stage of childhood, and moral judgment during the second.

It is most important to bear in mind the pictorial element in the period between the change of teeth and puberty. Artistic presentation is essential in teaching and education.[1] Painting, music, and perhaps modeling as well, must all find their proper place in education in order to satisfy the inherent longings of children.

Children's Relationship to the Earth

In other subjects we must also work according to these needs, not according to the demands of our materialistic age. Our materialistic age has fine things to tell us—for example, about how to distinguish one plant from another—but during this second stage, the teacher must know, above all, that the scientific method of classification and descriptions of individual plants does not belong in the education of children of this age. You must ask yourself whether a plant is, in effect, a reality. Can you understand a plant in isolation? This is impossible. Suppose you found a hair; you would not try to determine how this hair could have formed all by itself. It must have been pulled out or fallen out of someone's head. You can think of it as a reality only in relation to the whole organism. The hair is nothing on its own and cannot be understood that way. It is a sin against one's sense of reality to describe a hair in isolation, and it is just as much a sin against our sense of reality to describe a plant as an isolated unit.

---

1. The German word *bildlich* refers not only to the pictorial, but also to modeling, building, and art.

It may seem fantastic, but plants are in fact the "hair" of the living Earth. Just as you can understand what a hair is really like only when you consider how it grows out of the head—actually out of the whole organism—so in teaching about nature you must show the children how the Earth exists in a most intimate relationship to the world of plants. You must begin with the soil and, in this way, evoke an image of Earth as a living being. Just as people have hair on their head, the Earth as a living being has the plants on it. You should never consider the plants apart from the soil. You must never show the children a plucked flower as something real, since it has no reality of its own. A plant can no more exist without the soil than a hair can exist without the human organism. The essential thing in your teaching is to arouse the feeling in the child that this is so.

When children have the feeling that the Earth has some formation or another, and from this arises one or another blossom in the plant—when in fact they really experience the Earth as a living organism—they will gain the proper and true relationship to the human being and to the whole great Earth spread out before them. One would never arrive at this view by considering the plants in isolation from the Earth.

Children will be capable of acquiring the right view (which I have characterized in a somewhat abstract way) at about ten years of age. This may be seen through intimately observing what develops in a child. But up to this age, our teaching about plants—springing as they do from the living body of the Earth—must be in the form of an image. We should clothe it in fairy tales, in pictures, and in legends. Only after the tenth year, when the child begins to feel like an independent personality, can we speak of plants individually. Before then, a child does not discriminate between the self and the environment. The I is not completely separated from the surrounding world.

So we must speak of plants as though they were little human beings or little angels, we must make them feel and act like human beings, and we must do the same thing with the animals. Only later in school life do we speak of them objectively as separate units.

You must not pass too abruptly from one thing to another, however; for the true reality of the living Earth from which the plants spring has another side to show us—the animal realm. Animals are typically studied by placing one beside the other, dividing them into classes and species according to their similarities. At best, one speaks of the more perfect as having developed from the less perfected, and so on. In this way, however, we fail to bring the human being into any relationship with the environment. When you study animal forms without preconceptions, it soon becomes clear that there are essential differences in the nature of, for example, a lion and a cow.

When you observe a cow you find in her a one-sided development of what in human beings is the digestive system. The cow is completely a system of digestion, and all the other organs act as appendages more or less. This is why it is so interesting to watch a cow chewing the cud; she lies on the meadow and digests her food with great enthusiasm, such bodily enthusiasm. She is all digestion. Just watch her and you will see how the substances pass over from her stomach to the other parts of her body. You can see from her sense of ease and comfort, from the whole soul quality of the cow, how all this comes about.

Now look at the lion. Do you not feel that, if your own heart were not prevented by your intellect from pressing too heavily into the limbs, your own heart would be as warm as that of the lion? The lion is a one-sided development of the human breast quality; the lion's other organs are merely appendages. Or consider birds. We can see that a bird is really entirely head. Everything else about a bird is stunted; it is all head. I have chosen these particularly striking examples, but you can discover that every animal embodies some aspect of humankind in a one-sided way.

In the human being everything is brought into harmony; each organ is developed so that it is modulated and harmonized by the other organs. For animals, however, each species embodies one of these human qualities in a specialized way. What would the human nose be like if it were not held in check by the rest of the organization? You can find certain animals with highly developed noses. What would the human mouth become if it were free and were not subdued by the other organs? So you find in all animal forms a one-sided development of some part of the human being.

In ancient times, humankind had an instinctive knowledge of these things, but that has been forgotten in our materialistic era. At the beginning of the nineteenth century, echoes of such knowledge could still be found, but now we must come to it anew. Schelling, for example, based himself on an old tradition in his sense that an animal form lives in every human organ, and he made a rather extraordinary statement: What, he asked, is the human tongue? The human tongue is a "cuttlefish." The cuttlefish found in the sea is a tongue developed in a one-sided way. In this statement there is something that can really bring us knowledge of our relationship to the animal world spread out before us.

It is really true that—once you have detached this from the abstract form in which I have presented it to you, when you have grasped it inwardly and transformed it into a picture—it will link in a wonderful way to fables and stories about animals. If you have previously told children stories in which animals act like humans, now you can divide the human being into the entire animal kingdom. In this way you can move beautifully from one to the other.

Thus, we get two kinds of feeling in children. One is aroused by the plant world and wanders over the fields and meadows gazing at the plants. The child muses: "Below me is the living Earth, living its life in the plant realm, which gives me such delight. I am looking at something beyond myself that belongs to the Earth." Just as a child gets a deep, inner feeling that the plant world belongs to the Earth—as indeed it does—so also the child deeply feels the true relationship between the human and the animal world—the human being built up by a harmonization of the whole animal kingdom spread out over the Earth.

Thus, in natural history children see their own relationship to the world, and the connection between the living Earth and what springs forth from it. Poetic feelings are awakened, imaginative feelings that were slumbering in the child. In this way, a child is truly led through the feelings to find a place in the universe, and the subject of natural history at this age can be something that leads the child to moral experiences.

It is really true that education cannot consist of external rules and techniques, but must arise from a true knowledge of the human being; this will lead to experiencing oneself as a part of the world. And this experience of belonging to the world is what must be brought to children by educators.

Lecture Five

BERN, APRIL 17, 1924

Three Divisions in the Middle Period of Childhood

When we consider the time from the change of teeth to puberty (this important period really sets the standard for our education as a whole), we see that it is divided again into smaller stages. During the first of these, up to the ninth year, children are not in a position to distinguish clearly between self and the outside world; even in the feeling life, the experience of the world as distinguished from I-being is unclear. People today do not generally regard these things correctly. They may observe that a child bumps into the corner of a table and then immediately strikes the table. People then say, "This child thinks the table is alive, and because of this, the child hits it in return." People speak in terms of "animism" as they do in relation to cultural history, but in reality this is not the situation.

If you look into the child's soul you can see that the table is not seen as alive; not even living things are considered to be alive as they will be later on. But, just as children see their arms and hands as members of their own being, they view what occurs beyond the self as a continuation of their own being. Children do not yet distinguish between self and world. Consequently, during this stage—the first third of the time between change of teeth and puberty—we must bring everything to the child through fairy tales and legends so that, in everything children see, they will find something that is not separate, but a continuation of their own being.

From a developmental standpoint, the transition from the ninth to the tenth year is vitally important for children, though the precise moment varies from child to child, sometimes earlier, sometimes later. You will notice that around this time, children grow somewhat restless; they come to the teacher with questioning eyes, and these things require that you have a fine feeling. Children will ask things that startle you, very different from anything they had asked before. Children find themselves in a strange situation inwardly. Now it is not a question of giving them all sorts of admonitions in a pedantic and stilted way; it is our task, above all, to feel our way into their own being.

At this stage, something appears in the subconscious being of a child. It is not, of course, anything that the child could express consciously, but we may characterize it in this way: until this time, children unquestioningly accepted as truth, goodness, and beauty whatever the authority, or revered teacher, presented as true, good, and beautiful. They were completely devoted to the one who was their authority. But at this point between the ninth and tenth year something comes over children—in the feelings, not in thinking, since they do not yet intellectualize things. Something comes over them, and it awakens in the soul as a kind of faint, dreamlike question: How does the teacher know this? Where does it come from? Is my teacher really the world? Until now, my teacher was the world, but now there is a question: Does not the world go beyond the teacher?

Up to this point, the teacher's soul was transparent, and the child saw through it into the world; but now this adult has become increasingly opaque, and the child asks, out of the feelings, what justifies one thing or another. The teacher's whole bearing must then very tactfully find what is right for the child. It is not a matter of figuring out ahead of time what to say, but of knowing how to adapt to the situation with inner tact. If right at this moment one can find the appropriate thing for the child through an inner, imperceptible sympathy, it will have an immense significance for that child's whole life right up to the time of death. If a child at this stage of inner life can say of the teacher, "This person's words arise from the secrets and mysteries of the world," this will be of great value to the child. This is an essential aspect of our teaching method.

Cause and Effect and Education as a Healing Art

At this point in life, children experience the difference between the world and the I-being. Now you can progress from teaching about plants, as I described yesterday, to teaching about animals. If you do this as I described it, you will make the correct approach to a child's feeling for the world. Only in the third period—beginning between the middle of the eleventh year and toward the twelfth—will a child acquire any under-standing for what we might call a "feeling of causality." Prior to the twelfth year, you can speak to children as cleverly as you like about cause and effect, but you will find them blind to causality at that age. Just as the term *color-blind* is coined from color, we may coin the term *cause-blind.* Connections between cause and effect are not formed in the human being before the twelfth year. Therefore, it is only at this age that we can begin to teach children what they need to know about the physical, mineral realm, which of course involves physics and chemistry, thus going beyond a purely pictorial presentation. Before that age, not only would it be useless but would in fact be harmful.

This also shows us how to approach history lessons. Initially, history should be presented in terms of individual figures through a kind of "painting" of the soul, if I may call it that. Until a child's twelfth year, you should give the children only living pictures. Anything else would harden their being—it would bring about a kind of sclerosis of the soul. If before the eleventh year you speak to children of the way one epoch prepared another through certain impulses and so on, you create in them a sclerosis of the soul. People who have an eye for such things often see old men and women who learned about cause and effect in history much too early. This can even go into the physical body at this age through the same principles I have described. Physical sclerosis in old people can be traced back to, among other causes, the fact that they were taught too much about causality as children.

We must notice such connections and understand them. They constitute a demand of our civilization and lead us back to what could at one time be found through an instinctive knowledge of human nature—a knowledge that we can no longer use in these times of conscious thought. If we go back to earlier eras, however, even only as far as the early Greek times, we find that the words *educator* and *healer* were very closely related to each other, because people knew that when human beings enter this earthly life they have not yet reached their full height; they are beings who have yet to be brought to their highest potential.

This is why the idea of the Fall has such validity—that souls really enter earthly existence as subhuman beings. If they were not subhuman, we not need to educate them any more than we must educate a spider so that later on it can make a web. Human beings must be educated because they must be brought into their full humanity. And if you have the proper idea of how we must lead a person in body, soul, and spirit to become truly human, you will see that this must be done according to the same principles that bring an abnormal human being back to the right path. In the same way, ordinary education has the task of healing a person whose humanity has been injured. Only when we recognize again the natural and spiritual relationship between these two activities will we be able to fructify our education properly through an ethical physiology.

It is extraordinary to think how recently—and how thoroughly—these ideas have been lost. For example, Herder's *Reflections on the Philosophy of the History of Mankind* (1791) describes with real inner devotion how illness can teach one to observe the inner human being.[1] When people become ill, it is an attack on their normal course of being, and the way an illness manifests and how it leaves a person demonstrate the laws of human nature. Herder is delighted to discover that through instances of mental as well as of physical illness, he can learn about the inner structure of the human being. He is still clearly aware of the relationship between medicine and pedagogy. It is not so long ago, then, when the old principle still applied—the principle that when a human being enters the world, it is really due to illness caused by sin, and we must heal, or educate, that individual. Admittedly, this is expressed somewhat in the extreme, but there is real truth at its basis. This must be recognized as a demand of contemporary civilization, so that the widespread practice of creating abstractions, which has even penetrated education, will end, and so that we can truly move away from the things I have seen practiced.

Recently, I had to show a man round the Waldorf school, a man who had an important position in the world of education. We discussed the specifics of several pupils, and then this man summarized what he had observed in a somewhat strange way. He said, "If this is what we need to do, then teachers should study medicine." I replied that such an absolute judgment was unjustified. If it becomes necessary to bring a certain amount of medical knowledge to education, then we must do it. But it

---

1. Johann Gottfried Herder (1744–1803) was an important figure in the literary life of Germany during the 18th century. He was one of the first to break from the intellectual "Age of Enlightenment" and, as an "organic" philosopher of mind, art, and history, helped to prepare the way for the Romantic movement of the late 18th century. When Goethe was a student in Strasbourg he was greatly influenced by him.

is impossible to rely on old traditions and decide that one thing or another must apply. It will happen; it will become a requirement of society that "cultural medicine" and "cultural pedagogy" be brought closer together so they become mutually more beneficial. In many ways, everything that is currently needed is troublesome and awkward, but even life itself has become increasingly troublesome, and the cure will also be a troublesome matter.

In any case, teaching about minerals should, in practice, begin only between the eleventh and twelfth year, and history should also be treated only pictorially before then. During the eleventh or twelfth year, you can begin to consider cause and effect by connecting the various historical eras, and thus present children with a comprehensive survey. You will be able to observe the correctness of this method in this way: If you present causality in describing historical processes too soon, you will find that children do not listen; but if you do it at the proper time, they meet you with inner joy and eager participation.

Indeed, it is impossible to teach anything at all without a child's inner cooperation. In all education, we must bear in mind how a child will enter life at puberty.[2] Of course, there are also those young ladies and gentlemen who continue their education, and in the Waldorf school we have a university standard, with twelve classes that take them on to their eighteenth or nineteenth year or even farther. But even with these children, we must recognize that after puberty they really do go out into life, and our relationship to those students must be very different from what it was before. We must make every effort to educate in such a way that the intellect, which awakens at puberty, can then find nourishment in the child's own nature.

---

2. In Germany, unless a student was expected to go to a university, a young person would end academic training at around puberty and enter a technical school.

If during the early school years children have stored up an inner treasury of riches through imitation, through a feeling for authority, and from the pictorial nature of the teaching, then at puberty those inner riches can be transformed into intellectual activity. From that point on, the individual will be faced with the task of *thinking* what was willed and felt previously. And we must take the very greatest care that this intellectual thinking does not manifest too early; for a human being can experience freedom only when, rather than being poured in by teachers, the intellect can awaken from within on its own. It must not awaken in an impoverished soul, however. If there is nothing present in a person's inner being that was acquired through imitation and imagery—something that can rise into thinking from deep in the soul—then, as thinking develops at puberty, that individual will be unable to find the inner resources to progress; thinking would reach only into an emptiness. Such a person will find no anchorage in life; and at the very time when a person should really have found a certain inner sense of security, there will be a tendency to chase trivialities. During these awkward years, adolescents will imitate many things that seem pleasant (usually they are not exactly what would please their elders, who have a more utilitarian perspective); they imitate these things now, because they were not allowed to imitate in an appropriate and living way as younger children. Consequently, we see many young people after puberty wandering around looking for security in one thing or another, thus numbing their experience of inner freedom.

Educating for All of Life and Beyond

In every stage of life we must make sure that we do not educate only for that stage, but educate for all of a person's earthly life—and, in fact, beyond. People can arrive most beautifully at an understanding of their own immortal human being; after puberty, they can experience for themselves how what poured into their soul as images through imitation is now freed from the soul and rises into spirit. People can feel how it continues to work, from time into eternity, passing through birth and death. It is exactly this welling up of what was instilled in the human soul through the proper education that provides an inner experience of immortality; primarily, it is life experience itself that shows us we had existence before coming down into the physical world. And what the child takes in as picture and imitates through religious feeling, unites with what that child was before descending into the physical realm; thus an inner experience of the kernel of immortality arises.

I use the word *immortality,* which is in current use; but even though people still believe in it, it is really only half of the question. When we speak of immortality today, we do so out of a certain self-centeredness; it is true, of course, because it represents the fact that we do not perish at death, but that our life continues. But we fail to mention the other side—the "unborn." In ancient times, those who possessed an instinctive spiritual knowledge still recognized the two sides of eternity— the *undying* and the *unborn.* We will understand eternity only when we are able to understand both of these concepts. Eternity will be experienced when children are properly educated. Here again we are confronted by something where materialism should not be considered theoretically.

As I have already shown you, it is bad enough that all kinds of monists go around spreading various materialistic theories. But that is not in any sense the worst. The least harmful is what people only think; the worst is what flows into life to become life itself. And since the art of education has also fallen into the clutches of materialistic thinking, children are unable to experience the things I have mentioned—the experience of time passing into eternity. In this way, they lose their relationship to the eternal aspect of their own being. You can preach as much materialism as you like to those who have been correctly educated, and it will not affect them greatly. They will reply, "I have the sense that I am immortal, and unfortunately this is something that you and your proofs have overlooked."

It is always a matter of comprehending life itself, and not merely the thoughts. Furthermore, this may seem contradictory, but an indication and a symptom of the materialism of our present age is the very fact that people today are so eager for theories and world philosophies based on ideas and concepts. If we really perceive spirit, we never leave matter. If you pursue your study of anthroposophy, you will see how it makes its way into psychology and physiology, how it speaks of material things and processes in every detail. Anthroposophic physiology addresses the activity of the liver, the spleen, or the lung very differently from today's abstract physiology.

Abstract physiology thinks it sees the facts, but it really views facts in the same way a man might who, for example, finds a magnet. He does not know what it is, nor what forces are concealed within it, but he finds the magnet while with a woman who knows what a magnet is. He says to himself, "I'll take this home; it will make a good horseshoe." The woman says, "You can't use that as a horseshoe; that is a magnet." But the man only laughs.

Similarly, a natural scientist laughs when one speaks of the spiritual basis of the liver, spleen, or heart—if one says that spirit in fact lives within those organs. But people who laugh at such things can never deeply enter the reality of material substance. The most harmful aspect of materialism is not that it fails to understand spirit. That will be corrected eventually. The worst thing about materialism is that it is completely ignorant of matter and its activity, because it fails to find spirit in matter.

There was never a time when people knew less about matter than they do now; for you cannot find material substance in the human being without a knowledge of spirit. Consequently, I would say that the error of materialism in education is demonstrated in life when people have no feeling or inner experience of their own eternal nature. If a person has been educated in the right way—that is, if the principles of the education have been read from human nature itself—death will be experienced as an event in life and not merely its end. In this way, one learns that in the relationship between teacher and child (and later between the teacher and the young man or woman) there are not only external things at work; even in the very small child, as I have already told you, intangible forces are at work—things we can neither see nor weigh and measure.

Punishment in the Classroom

We must bear this in mind when we consider punishment as a means of education. (A question was raised in regard to this.) We cannot simply ask ourselves whether or not we should punish. How can we possibly deal with all the mischievous things children do if we completely eliminate punishment? The question of whether to punish or not is really an individual matter. Various methods can be used with some children, whereas others may respond only to punishment. The manner of punishment, however, really depends on the teacher's temperament.

We must remember that we are not dealing with carved wooden figures but with human beings. Teachers must consider their own nature, as well as the nature of the children. The important thing is not so much *what* we do, but *how*—that the only effective punishment is inflicted by a teacher with complete inner calm and deliberation. If a punishment arises from anger, it will be completely ineffective. Here, of course, a teacher can accomplish a great deal through self-development.

Otherwise, something like this may happen: A girl makes a mess, and the boy next to her gets upset with her. The teacher then begins to scold the boy, saying, "You should not get angry like that! The child replies, "But grown-up people get angry when unpleasant things happen to them." Then the teacher says, "If you get angry I'll throw something at you!"

If you punish in anger this way, you may get a scene like this: a teacher comes into a classroom of fairly young children who are playing. She says, "What an awful commotion you are all making! What are you doing? Why are you shouting and making so much noise?" Finally one child gets up enough courage to say, "You are the only one shouting." Now, in terms of punishment or admonition, everything depends on the soul mood of the one punishing or admonishing. Whenever a child has done something very naughty, you can even take the precaution of ignoring it for the time being; you could sleep on it and take it up again the next day. At least in this way you may find the necessary inner calm, and however you decide to deal with that child, your admonition or your punishment will be far more effective than anything you do while angry. This method may have its drawbacks as well, but you must always weigh one thing against another and not become too one-sided.

"Reading" the Child

You can see that in this method of teaching and education, based as it is on anthroposophic principles, each particular age of the child must be read, as it were. We must see more in a human being than present scientific thinking wants to see. Of course, such scientific thinking has contributed to wonderful progress, but in terms of human beings, it is as though they had something written in front of them and began to describe the letters of that writing. It is certainly useful and beautiful to have the letters described, but that is not the point; we must *read.* We do not need to describe the organs and how the soul works in them, which is the modern method, but we must have the capacity to read the human being. Such "reading" for a teacher may be understood by imagining that you have a book in your hand, and, no matter how interesting it may be, if you cannot read it but only look at the printed letters, it will not arouse you very strongly to any inner activity. If, for example, someone has a very interesting novel, but can only describe the letters, then nothing will happen within that person. So it is with the art of education—nothing happens in a person who merely describes the individual organs or the various aspects of the human soul. Educators who can read will find in every child a "book of the soul."

Children can become reading material of the soul for their teachers, even in very large classes. If this happens, a teacher will sense when, before the ninth or tenth year, children do not differentiate between the world and their own I-being; they will sense how, before this time, children are unable, out of themselves, to write anything in the way of a composition. At most, they will be able to retell something they have heard in fairy tales or legends. Only when children are nine or ten can you gradually begin to present images and thoughts that they can in turn write about from their own free feelings and ideas. The inner thought structure needed by a child before being able to write an essay is not yet present before the twelfth year; they should not be encouraged to write essays before then. (I am speaking of this, because someone asked about it.) If they do this too soon, they will begin to suffer not from "sclerosis" of the soul in this case, but from "rickets" of the soul. Later in life, such a child will become inwardly weak and ineffective.

Only when our study of the human being can lead us to an a unique knowledge of each child will we be able to educate them in the appropriate way; the correct education must enable children to take their place socially in the everyday world. Indeed, children belong to this world, and must enter more and more deeply into it as long as they live on Earth; and after death they will be able to live on properly in the spiritual realm. This experience is indeed a real condition for life in the world beyond the gate of death.

The Capacity to Meet Other Human Beings

Human beings become hardened when they cannot discover how to meet other people in a truly human way; they harden themselves for the life that will face them after death. People have lost the capacity for meeting one another in a human way, and this is yet another dark side to the picture of our time. Nowhere do we find people who can enter with loving feeling into another human being. This is clearly evident due to the amount of talk about social demands these days. Why is this?

The obvious basis of social life—the power to truly feel and experience with another person—has been sadly lost. Whenever demands are urgently presented in any given age, those very demands show us what is missing in that time, because whatever people lack, they demand. Real social life is missing, and this is why the social ideal is so vehemently discussed in our current era. But education for social life is hardly touched, although many enlightened people speak of it. It has retreated increasingly into the background, and in many respects, human beings meet and pass each other without any understanding of one another.

It is indeed a grievous feature of present-day life that when one human being meets another, there is no mutual understanding. You can find clubs and societies with one or another common aim, where people have worked together for years, but they really do not know each other at all. People know nothing about the inner life of those they work with, because they lack a living interest, a living devotion, a living sympathy in relation to the other. But such living interest, devotion, and sympathy will be present if, at the right age, we permeate every area of teaching and education with the principle of imitation and, in its proper place, the principle of authority. This social feeling and understanding for others depends, in a most intimate way, on whether or not we have any sense of what in our world participates in the spiritual realm.

There was a time when human beings knew very little about the Earth; the tools they used were simple and primitive, and the way they represented natural objects in art was sometimes very talented but remarkably undeveloped. We now live in an age when we use complicated tools to master nature, and the most minute details are painstakingly copied, for example, in our works of art. But what we lack today is the power to enter the spirit of nature, the spirit of the cosmos, and the universe as a grand whole. That power must be reclaimed.

Above all, in the astronomical realm we have lost sight of our relationship to the universe. If you look at a plant, you can see how it takes root in the ground—how it arises from a seed, unfolds its first leaves and stem, more leaves and a blossom, and how it then gathers itself together again in the fruit. Goethe described it this way: In the plant you see how it draws out into space, rotates, and then contracts. Goethe was unable to go far enough. He described this expansion and contraction of the plant, but could not come to the point of knowing why this happens. It happens because the plant is exposed to the forces of the Moon and Sun. Whenever the Sun's forces are active, the plant expands and opens its leaves; when Moon forces act on it, plant life contracts—it develops the stem and then the seed, where the whole plant life is drawn together in a single point. Thus, when we consider this expansion and contraction as Goethe has shown it to us, we see in it the alternation of Sun and Moon forces, and we are led out into the distant spaces of the cosmos. When we can see how the stars are at work in the plant, we do not remain bound and limited.

These Sun and Moon forces that influence plants act in a more complicated way on the human being, and this leads us to think that the human being is not just a citizen of Earth, but of the cosmos as well. We know that when we eat—for example, cabbage or venison—or drink something, whatever relates to life pursues its own course within us. We nevertheless know about such things, because can perceive them. But we have no knowledge of how we are connected with the starry worlds in our soul and spirit—how the forces of contraction live in the sphere of the Moon, the forces of expansion in that of the Sun; we do not know that these forces maintain the balance more or less perfectly in a human being—that melancholic tendencies have their roots in the Moon realm, sanguine tendencies of soul in the Sun, and balance and harmony are brought about by cosmic activity.

A detailed discussion of this in no way diminishes our concept of freedom, nor does it lead to preposterous ideas of any kind. This can all be examined with the same precision used in mathematics. But mathematics, though true, remains abstract. The knowledge of Sun and Moon that I mentioned leads us to see how we receive spiritual nourishment from what flows from the whole galaxy of stars; it becomes a strength within us, a driving force. If we can unite in this way with the spirit of the universe, we will become whole human beings, and the urge will no longer arise to bypass others without understanding, but as true human beings we will find the true human being in others. The more we describe only matter and apply those descriptions to human beings, the more we freeze the life of the soul; but if we can ally ourselves with the spirit, we can serve our fellow human beings with true warmth of heart. Thus, an education that seeks and finds the spirit in the person will lay the foundations for human love, human sympathy, and human service in the proper sense of the word.

In an organism, everything is at the same time a beginning and an end; this is also true of the whole life of the spirit. You can never know the world without practicing a knowledge of the human being—without looking into the self. For the human being is a mirror of the world; all the secrets of the universe are contained in the human being. The fixed stars work in the human being, the moving planets work in the human being, and all the elements of nature work there as well. To understand the human being—to see true being there—is also to find a place in the world in the right way.

Consequently, education must be permeated by a kind of golden rule that quickens all the teacher's work with the children, something that gives life to that work, just as, in a physical sense, the blood gives life to the physical organism. So out of a worldview permeated with spirit, the lifeblood of the soul must enter the soul of the teacher. Then the soul's lifeblood will set its imprint on all the methods and practice of the teaching effort and save them from becoming abstract principles. Something will thus live in the educator, which I would like to characterize through these concluding words, as a kind of education for life itself:

> To spend oneself in matter
> is to grind down souls.
>
> To find oneself in the spirit
> is to unite human beings.
>
> To see oneself in all humanity
> is to construct worlds.

Further Reading

Essential Works by Rudolf Steiner

Anthroposophical Leading Thoughts: Anthroposophy as a Path of Knowledge: The Michael Mystery, Rudolf Steiner Press, London, 1985.

Anthroposophy (A Fragment), Anthroposophic Press, Hudson, NY, 1996.

An Autobiography, Steinerbooks, Blauvelt, NY, 1977.

Christianity as Mystical Fact, Anthroposophic Press, Hudson, NY, 1997.

The Foundation Stone / The Life, Nature, and Cultivation of Anthroposophy, Rudolf Steiner Press, London, 1996.

How to Know Higher Worlds: A Modern Path of Initiation, Anthroposophic Press, Hudson, NY, 1994.

Intuitive Thinking as a Spiritual Path: A Philosophy of Freedom, Anthroposophic Press, Hudson, NY, 1995 (previously translated as *Philosophy of Spiritual Activity*).

An Outline of Esoteric Science, Anthroposophic Press, Hudson, NY, 1997 (previous translation titled *An Outline of Occult Science*).

A Road to Self-Knowledge and The Threshold of the Spiritual World, Rudolf Steiner Press, London, 1975.

Theosophy: An Introduction to the Spiritual Processes in Human Life and in the Cosmos, Anthroposophic Press, Hudson, NY, 1994.

Books by Other Authors

Anschütz, Marieke. *Children and Their Temperaments*, Floris Books, Edinburgh, 1995.

Barnes, Henry. *A Life for the Spirit: Rudolf Steiner in the Crosscurrents of Our Time*. Anthroposophic Press, Hudson, NY, 1997.

Britz-Crecelius, Heidi. *Children at Play: Using Waldorf Principles to Foster Childhood Development*, Park Street Press, Rochester, VT, 1996.

Budd, Christopher Houghton (ed). *Rudolf Steiner, Economist: Articles & Essays*, New Economy Publications, Canterbury, UK, 1996.

Carlgren, Frans. *Education Towards Freedom: Rudolf Steiner Education: A Survey of the Work of Waldorf Schools Throughout the World*, Lanthorn Press, East Grinstead, England, 1993.

Childs, Gilbert. *Education and Beyond: Steiner and the Problems of Modern Society*, Floris Books, Edinburgh, 1996.

—— *Understanding Your Temperament! A Guide to the Four Temperaments*, Sophia Books, London, 1995.

Childs, Dr. Gilbert and Sylvia Childs. *Your Reincarnating Child*, Sophia Books/Rudolf Steiner Press, London, 1995.

Edmunds, L. Francis. *Renewing Education: Selected Writings on Steiner Education*, Hawthorn Press, Stroud, UK, 1992.

——*Rudolf Steiner Education: The Waldorf School*, Rudolf Steiner Press, London, 1992.

Fenner, Pamela Johnson and Karen L. Rivers, eds. *Waldorf Student Reading List*, third edition, Michaelmas Press, Amesbury, MA, 1995.

Finser, Torin M. *School as a Journey: The Eight-Year Odyssey of a Waldorf Teacher and His Class*, Anthroposophic Press, Hudson, NY, 1994.

Gabert, Erich. *Educating the Adolescent: Discipline or Freedom*, Anthroposophic Press, Hudson, NY, 1988.

Gardner, John Fentress. *Education in Search of the Spirit: Essays on American Education*, Anthroposophic Press, Hudson, NY, 1996.

—— *Youth Longs to Know: Explorations of the Spirit in Education*, Anthroposophic Press, Hudson, NY, 1997.

Gatto, John Taylor. *Dumbing Us Down: The Hidden Curriculum of Compulsory Schooling*, New Society, Philadelphia, 1992.

Harwood, A. C. *The Recovery of Man in Childhood: A Study in the Educational Work of Rudolf Steiner*, The Myrin Institute of New York, New York, 1992.

Heider, Molly von. *Looking Forward: Games, rhymes and exercises to help children develop their learning abilities*, Hawthorn Press, Stroud, UK, 1995.

Heydebrand, Caroline von, *Childhood: A Study of the Growing Child*, Anthroposophic Press, Hudson, NY, 1995.

Jaffke, Freya. *Work and Play in Early Childhood*, Anthroposophic Press, Hudson, NY, 1996.

Large, Martin. *Who's Bringing Them Up? How to Break the T.V. Habit!* Hawthorn Press, Stroud, UK, 1990.

Logan, Arnold, ed. *A Garden of Songs for Singing and Piping at Home and School*, Windrose Publishing and Educational Services, Chatham, NY, 1996.

McDermott, Robert. *The Essential Steiner: Basic Writings of Rudolf Steiner.* Harper Collins, New York, 1984.

Maher, Stanford and Yvonne Bleach. *"Putting the Heart Back into Teaching": A Manual for Junior Primary Teachers*, Novalis Press, Cape Town, South Africa, 1996.

Maher, Stanford and Ralph Shepherd. *Standing on the Brink—An Education for the 21st Century: Essays on Waldorf Education*, Novalis Press, Cape Town, South Africa, 1995.

Nobel, Agnes. *Educating through Art: The Steiner School Approach*, Floris Books, Edinburgh, 1996.

Pusch, Ruth, ed. *Waldorf Schools Volume I: Kindergarten and Early Grades*, Mercury Press, Spring Valley, NY, 1993.

—— *Waldorf Schools Volume II: Upper Grades and High School*, Mercury Press, Spring Valley, NY, 1993.

Richards, M. C. *Opening Our Moral Eye*, Lindisfarne Books, Hudson, NY, 1996.

Spock, Marjorie. *Teaching as a Lively Art*, Anthroposophic Press, Hudson, NY, 1985.

THE FOUNDATIONS
OF WALDORF EDUCATION

THE FIRST FREE WALDORF SCHOOL opened its doors in Stuttgart, Germany, in September, 1919, under the auspices of Emil Molt, the Director of the Waldorf Astoria Cigarette Company and a student of Rudolf Steiner's spiritual science and particularly of Steiner's call for social renewal.

It was only the previous year—amid the social chaos following the end of World War I—that Emil Molt, responding to Steiner's prognosis that truly human change would not be possible unless a sufficient number of people received an education that developed the whole human being, decided to create a school for his workers' children. Conversations with the minister of education and with Rudolf Steiner, in early 1919, then led rapidly to the forming of the first school.

Since that time, more than six hundred schools have opened around the globe—from Italy, France, Portugal, Spain, Holland, Belgium, Great Britain, Norway, Finland, and Sweden to Russia, Georgia, Poland, Hungary, Romania, Israel, South Africa, Australia, Brazil, Chile, Peru, Argentina, Japan, and others—making the Waldorf school movement the largest independent school movement in the world. The United States, Canada, and Mexico alone now have more than 120 schools.

Although each Waldorf school is independent, and although there is a healthy oral tradition going back to the first Waldorf teachers and to Steiner himself, as well as a growing body of secondary literature, the true foundations of the Waldorf method and spirit remain the many lectures that Rudolf Steiner gave on the subject. For five years (1919–24), Rudolf Steiner, while simultaneously working on many other fronts, tirelessly dedicated himself to the dissemination of the idea of Waldorf education. He gave manifold lectures to teachers, parents, the general public, and even the children themselves. New schools were founded. The movement grew.

While many of Steiner's foundational lectures have been translated and published in the past, some have never appeared in English, and many have been virtually unobtainable for years. To remedy this situation and to establish a coherent basis for Waldorf education, Anthroposophic Press has decided to publish the complete series of Steiner lectures and writings on education in a uniform series. This series will thus constitute an authoritative foundation for work in educational renewal, for Waldorf teachers, parents, and educators generally.

RUDOLF STEINER'S LECTURES
(AND WRITINGS) ON EDUCATION

I. *Allgemeine Menschenkunde als Grundlage der Pädagogik. Pädagogischer Grundkurs,* 14 Lectures, Stuttgart, 1919 (GA 293). Previously *Study of Man. The Foundations of Human Experience* (Anthroposophic Press, 1996).

II. *Erziehungskunst Methodische-Didaktisches,* 14 Lectures, Stuttgart, 1919 (GA 294). *Practical Advice to Teachers* (Rudolf Steiner Press, 1988).

III. *Erziehungskunst,* 15 Discussions, Stuttgart, 1919 (GA 295). *Discussions with Teachers* (Anthroposophic Press, 1997).

IV. *Die Erziehungsfrage als soziale Frage,* 6 Lectures, Dornach, 1919 (GA 296). *Education as a Force for Social Change* (previously *Education as a Social Problem*) (Anthroposophic Press, 1997).

V. *Die Waldorf Schule und ihr Geist,* 6 Lectures, Stuttgart and Basel, 1919 (GA 297). *The Spirit of the Waldorf School* (Anthroposophic Press, 1995).

VI. *Rudolf Steiner in der Waldorfschule, Vorträge und Ansprachen,* Stuttgart, 1919–1924 (GA 298). *Rudolf Steiner in the Waldorf School: Lectures and Conversations* (Anthroposophic Press, 1996).

VII. *Geisteswissenschaftliche Sprachbetrachtungen,* 6 Lectures, Stuttgart, 1919 (GA 299). *The Genius of Language* (Anthroposophic Press, 1995).

VIII. *Konferenzen mit den Lehren der Freien Waldorfschule 1919–1924,* 3 Volumes (GA 300). *Conferences with Teachers* (Steiner Schools Fellowship, 1986, 1987, 1988, 1989).

IX. *Die Erneuerung der Pädagogisch-didaktischen Kunst durch Geisteswissenschaft,* 14 Lectures, Basel, 1920 (GA 301). *The Renewal of Education* (Kolisko Archive Publications for Steiner Schools Fellowship Publications, Michael Hall, Forest Row, East Sussex, UK, 1981).

X. *Menschenerkenntnis und Unterrichtsgestaltung,* 8 Lectures, Stuttgart, 1921 (GA 302). Previously *The Supplementary Course—Upper School* and *Waldorf Education for Adolescence. Education for Adolescents* (Anthroposophic Press, 1996).

XI. *Erziehung und Unterricht aus Menschenerkenntnis,* 9 Lectures, Stuttgart, 1920, 1922, 1923 (GA 302a). The first four lectures available as *Balance in Teaching* (Mercury Press, 1982); last three lectures as *Deeper Insights into Education* (Anthroposophic Press, 1988).

XII. *Die Gesunder Entwicklung des Menschenwesens,* 16 Lectures, Dornach, 1921–22 (GA 303). *Soul Economy and Waldorf Education* (Anthroposophic Press, 1986).

XIII. *Erziehungs- und Unterrichtsmethoden auf Anthroposophischer Grundlage,* 9 Public Lectures, various cities, 1921–22 (GA 304). *Waldorf Education and Anthroposophy 1* (Anthroposophic Press, 1995).

XIV. *Anthroposophische Menschenkunde und Pädagogik,* 9 Public Lectures, various cities, 1923–24 (GA 304a). *Waldorf Education and Anthroposophy 2* (Anthroposophic Press, 1996).

XV. *Die geistig-seelischen Grundkräfte der Erziehungskunst,* 12 Lectures, 1 Special Lecture, Oxford 1922 (GA 305). *The Spiritual Ground of Education* (Garber Publications, 1989).

XVI. *Die pädagogisch Praxis vom Gesichtspunkte geisteswissenschaftlicher Menschenerkenntnis,* 8 Lectures, Dornach, 1923 (GA 306). *The Child's Changing Consciousness As the Basis of Pedagogical Practice* (Anthroposophic Press, 1996).

XVII. *Gegenwärtiges Geistesleben und Erziehung,* 4 Lectures, Ilkeley, 1923 (GA 307). *A Modern Art of Education* (Rudolf Steiner Press, 1981) and *Education and Modern Spiritual Life* (Garber Publications, n.d.).

XVIII. *Die Methodik des Lehrens und die Lebensbedingungen des Erziehens,* 5 Lectures, Stuttgart, 1924 (GA 308). *The Essentials of Education* (Anthroposophic Press, 1997).

XIX. *Anthroposophische Pädagogik und ihre Voraussetzungen,* 5 Lectures, Bern, 1924 (GA 309). *The Roots of Education* (Anthroposophic Press, 1997).

XX. *Der pädagogische Wert der Menschenerkenntnis und der Kulturwert der Pädagogik,* 10 Public Lectures, Arnheim, 1924 (GA 310). *Human Values in Education* (Rudolf Steiner Press, 1971).

XXI. *Die Kunst des Erziehens aus dem Erfassen der Menschenwesenheit,* 7 Lectures, Torquay, 1924 (GA 311). *The Kingdom of Childhood* (Anthroposophic Press, 1995).

XXII. *Geisteswissenschaftliche Impulse zur Entwicklung der Physik. Erster naturwissenschaftliche Kurs: Licht, Farbe, Ton—Masse, Elektrizität, Magnetismus,* 10 Lectures, Stuttgart, 1919–20 (GA 320). *The Light Course* (Steiner Schools Fellowship,1977).

XXIII. *Geisteswissenschaftliche Impulse zur Entwicklung der Physik. Zweiter naturwissenschaftliche Kurs: die Wärme auf der Grenze positiver und negativer Materialität,* 14 Lectures, Stuttgart, 1920 (GA 321). *The Warmth Course* (Mercury Press, 1988).

XXIV. *Das Verhältnis der verschiedenen naturwissenschaftlichen Gebiete zur Astronomie. Dritter naturwissenschaftliche Kurs: Himmelskunde in Beziehung zum Menschen und zur Menschenkunde,* 18 Lectures, Stuttgart, 1921 (GA 323). Available in typescript only as "**The Relation of the Diverse Branches of Natural Science to Astronomy.**"

XXV. *The Education of the Child and Early Lectures on Education* (A collection) (Anthroposophic Press, 1996).

XXVI. Miscellaneous.

Index

DURING THE LAST TWO DECADES of the nineteenth
century the Austrian-born Rudolf Steiner (1861–1925)
became a respected and well-published scientific, literary, and
philosophical scholar, particularly known for his work on
Goethe's scientific writings. After the turn of the century he
began to develop his earlier philosophical principles into an
approach to methodical research of psychological and spiritual phenomena.

His multifaceted genius has led to innovative and holistic
approaches in medicine, philosophy, religion, education (Waldorf schools), special education, economics, agriculture (Bio-
dynamic method), science, architecture, drama, the new arts
of speech and eurythmy, and other fields of activity. In 1924
he founded the General Anthroposophical Society, which
today has branches throughout the world.

. . . .

*For an informative catalog of the work of Rudolf Steiner
and other anthroposophical authors please contact*

ANTHROPOSOPHIC PRESS
3390 Route 9, Hudson, NY 12534
TEL: 518-851-2054
FAX: 518-851-2047